CONTENTS

ACKNOWLEDGEMENTS

I would like to acknowledge the support and good deeds of a number of organisations and individuals who have played a very important part in my life.

MIND, Mencap and the National Council for Civil Liberties have worked with never-ending understanding and dedication to protect the rights of those who suffer from mental ill-health, and to help their families. The members of PROPAR, both activists and supporters, have given generously of their time and energy. With the help of MIND, Mencap and the NCCL, they have brought special hospitals into the public eye, and have begun to lead them out of the dark ages.

Without the legal assistance of my solicitor, Paul Bacon, and his understanding and social support, so freely given, I could have not resettled so successfully into society, nor could I have been so free today.

No words can describe the trust and respect I have for Ray. I thank this sincere man and his wife for their great kindness towards me.

Finally, but most important, I dedicate this book to my dear wife Jean who has given me the fulfilment of belonging I sought for so long.

FOREWORD

Born a Number is the story of one man's journey through many of the institutions we have designed for human beings who do not, or cannot, fit into an ordinary family structure. Leonard Harding started his institutional career at the age of one in a children's home in Shrewsbury, and finished it 36 years later when he was discharged from Eastdale, a rehabilitation unit for patients from the special hospitals.

At the centre of the story is Len Harding's account of his years in Rampton, one of the four special hospitals for people who need treatment for mental disorder under conditions of special security on account of their dangerous, violent or criminal propensities. His straightforward reminiscences of this period in his life are characterised by his complete openness and honesty. Where praise is due, it is given; where Len Harding experienced happiness, he says so; but when pain, brutality and inhuman treatment were his lot, he is not afraid to relive it. His unemotional and extraordinarily balanced account enables the reader to begin to comprehend the lives and experiences and, above all, the sense of powerlessness of people who, like Len Harding, are consigned to a system which appears to be designed for the benefit of nobody, least of all the people it is supposed to help.

At one level this book is about one man's life, and as such it stands on its own. At another level it asks, in a direct, poignant and yet unsentimental manner, whether the way we provide mental health care — especially in the special hospital system — can ever fulfil the objectives any civilised country should set for such institutions. Over the last 15 years the special hospitals have been the subject of numerous reports, of which the 1980 Boynton Report on Rampton Hospital was the most worrying.

In one sense this book is largely about the years leading up to that report. Five years have passed since Boynton highlighted Rampton's isolation from the rest of the NHS, the absence of an effective complaints system, lack of therapeutic direction, poor internal communications, staff tension and out-dated custodial attitudes. Since then a great deal of money has been spent on improving the fabric of institutions like Broadmoor and Rampton, greater openness to the outside world is very slowly becoming apparent and the first signs of a professional approach that is not dominated by custodianalism are appearing. And yet does it make sense to pour money into enormous institutions which remain administratively, professionally and geographically isolated, institutions from which it is still as difficult to be transferred as it was in the days when Len Harding was in Rampton, institutions which, apart from a few shining examples, offer patients little opportunity for social rehabilitation?

This is an important debate that will continue. Much has been written on it, especially recently, but almost all of the literature so far has been by professionals. **Born a Number** is one of the first books to be written by somebody who has experienced the system from the inside, and as such it fills in many of the gaps left by the professional literature. It is essential reading for consumers and their families, professionals, members of voluntary organisations and anybody else who cares about how we in Britain provide mental health care, especially care in conditions of security.

It is clear to us that new thinking and policy about caring for mentally disordered people in secure conditions must precede large financial outlays on old institutional structures. The time is right for government to undertake a systematic and critical review of the full range of secure provision. Ideas have emerged from MIND[1], the King's Fund Centre[2] and professionals themselves[3], ideas which have yet to evoke an appropriate response from government. Now we have a truly sensitive account of the special hospital system by a former patient. This book fills in the gaps in experience and sensitivity left by the professional literature and offers an insight which is essential for policy development; Len Harding's account of the secure mental health services is of a quality only a thoughtful user of the services could provide. All of those professionals and policy makers who *think* they know about the quality of life available to a patient in a secure institution should read this book for their own edification.

William Bingley

William Bingley
Assistant Director (Legal Services)
MIND

Larry Gostin

Larry Gostin
Director
Collaborative Centre for Health & Law
Harvard University School of Public Health

November 1985

References
1. MIND (1983) *Common Concern.*
2. GOSTIN, L. (1985) *Institutions Observed.* King's Fund Centre, London.
3. GOSTIN, L. (Ed) (1985) *Secure Provision: A Review of Special Services for the Mentally Ill and Mentally Handicapped in England and Wales.* Tavistock, London.

PREFACE

Did you know that one person in six will need some sort of treatment for mental ill-health? Or that the staff of some mental hospitals are bound by the Official Secrets Act?

Through lack of knowledge or interest — or both — most members of society take a very negative view of mental illness. They are given a false image by people who should know better.

This book has been written because I believe that the citizens of this country should know what is said and done in their name.

The names of people and places have been changed to protect those who are decent and caring from any indiscretions which might have been included.

LJH

1. STARTING OUT

FIRST MEMORIES

On 8 December 1941 a Canadian soldier and a 19-year-old English girl had an illegitimate son, as so many people did in those days of bitter conflict. The child was christened Leonard John Harding.

I wasn't wanted from the moment I was born, so it came as no surprise to find out much later in life that the police and the NSPCC took me away from my mother when I was one year old. I had been severely neglected, and was suffering from — amongst other things — congenital syphilis. I was treated for this by a course of injections, which were successful, and on leaving hospital I was placed in the care of the Church of England Children's Society. The Society sent me to a home for infants in Shrewsbury, and I stayed there until just before my sixth birthday.

In those days, children were allocated to homes according to their sex and age, and regular reports were made on their progress. These reports followed you and were kept up-to-date as you went to different homes. Early reports made at the Shrewsbury infants home suggested that I was mentally retarded and had speech defects. While there could be no mistake about my speech, to label such a young child who had been faced with problems from birth as mentally retarded could well create difficulties in the future.

I cannot recall any of the time I spent at Shrewsbury infants home, but I do remember very well being transferred from there to St Peter's Home in Malvern, Worcestershire. I particularly remember feeling so happy as I walked along Cowley Road with a welfare officer. The day was hot, the sky was blue, the Malvern Hills towered in the background: it seemed a very quiet and peaceful place. As we came to St Peter's the gate was open; we started to climb the steps and with every step I took the house seemed to get bigger. The door at the side of the huge house opened and a big woman appeared. I started to cry as I felt afraid, although I had no real reason to be. We were taken into a very well set out sitting room, and I sat close to the lady who had brought me to St Peter's because I was so frightened.

The home itself was three storeys high. The bottom floor consisted of the kitchen, scullery, storerooms, boilerhouse, toilets, laundry rooms, washroom, dayroom, clothing rooms, dining room and lounge. On the second floor were the Master and Matron's rooms, sitting rooms, office, storeroom, a big lounge (which was later turned into a TV lounge and a billiards room), toilets and bathrooms. The third floor consisted of the deputies' rooms, dormitories, toilets and bathrooms.

At the front of the house was a long winding drive with a lawn at the end and a huge playground. At the back was a big garden area and beyond that some woods.

St Peter's Home was run by Mr and Mrs Mullock and their deputies Mr and Mrs Trany. We called Mr Mullock *Master* and Mrs Mullock *Matron*, and we were allowed to call Mr and Mrs Trany *Uncle Roll* and *Auntie Joyce*. Mrs Mullock was a fair and just matron and the more I got to know her the more I began to trust and respect her, although for some unknown reason I never felt completely at ease when she was about. The Master I took to straight away. He was not a very healthy man, but his sense of humour and friendliness calmed me down. When he came into the room after the welfare lady had gone the Master made very realistic trumpet noises, which made me laugh and forget my fears. St Peter's was for male children only, and we had very little contact with any females apart from the Matron and Auntie Joyce. I met Michael in my first few days at the home, and he became my first friend: we stayed in touch for years after we left the orphanage.

Once the welfare lady had handed me over, I was taken into the dayroom to meet a couple of other lads and left there to play until the midday meal. I sat in the corner on a radiator and listened to the radio, and this became my favourite place. Even at this early age music had a special meaning for me, and to this day a good ballad or piano concerto fills me with happiness and a sense of peace.

I had a very good up-bringing at St Peter's in the sense that I was well cared for, but in some respects I suppose I had too good a life because I was cocooned. The daily routine was easy to remember. We would be woken at about 7.00 am each day, wash, change, and go into the dayroom until breakfast time. Lads in certain age groups had jobs to do like making beds or setting tables and cleaning up before and after meals. When breakfast was ready we would all gather in the dayroom for morning assembly. We would finish assembly by praying then move off line by line to the dining room. Meals were very good, in fact looking back I would say we were *too* well fed with four meals a day! After breakfast we would get ready for school.

All the lads would be back from school at 5.00 pm at the latest, change, wash, see to the cutlery and sit down to tea by about 5.30. After tea the youngest lads would be in bed by 6.15 and the older lads would be sent to bed between 8.00 and 9.00, apart from nights when there were cubs or scouts or for any other special reason.

The cub and scout huts were in the wood behind the house. Any of the lads from the home could join the local cubs or scouts when they reached the right age and I certainly enjoyed my time in the cubs. We were in an ideal area to practise skills such as tracking, nature walks and camping and to use crafts like knots and signals. I was very proud of my uniform, and the happiness I got from being in the local group will always stay with me.

Cubs and scouts meant a late night which didn't bother me as I never slept well. I hated bed in those days and even now I'm not keen — I'm up as soon as I'm awake. My bedroom in the home was directly above the Master and Matron's quarters and opposite Uncle Roll and Auntie Joyce's rooms. One night I woke up and to my horror found four cockroaches crawling over me. How I screamed — I shouted 'Mummy Mummy' — and I was so afraid until Matron appeared. She turned the light on and charged through the room like a dose of salts. God knows how long it was before I went back to sleep but she stayed with me all the time and at that moment I looked upon her as my mother. It was many years before I went to bed without the light on and without first looking all around the room.

My number at the home was the same number I had at my first school, number 12.

SCHOOLDAYS

My first day at St Peter's School was one I could hardly forget. I set off with my friend Micky and some other lads. St Peter's School was next to St Peter's Church, and as we passed the church we saw a group of boys and girls playing about in the hedge with a wasps nest. I had to be nosey, and of course I paid the price. I was stung just above the eye and ran all the way home, missing half the morning's schooling. After the sting had been seen to, the Master took me back to school in his car which was my first ride in a car. I enjoyed it, although it was only a quick ride.

I looked forward to going to school yet I was frightened, even though I had my friends Micky and Lewis in the same class and I enjoyed the morning assembly. At the home I had my corner and music for comfort when I felt lonely and frightened, but at school I felt out of place and alone.

In the years I spent at St Peter's School I had my mishaps like most kids do, for example being caned for something someone else had done, or being found out of bounds. However I had many happy times too and I couldn't understand why I was unable to learn. One of my favourite times was Wednesday morning when the Master would drive me to the speech therapist. After a few trips I noticed a white horse in the field next to the big laundry works on the main Worcester and Malvern road. Thereafter Snowy became 'my' horse, and we would stop and feed him sugar squares. While on these trips to the speech therapist I looked upon the Master as my own dad, and I was always a little sad when the time came for me to be dropped off back at school.

*   *   *

At weekends the routine changed at the home. Saturday was the day for your bath, haircut and a change of clothing, and then, depending on your number and how quickly you got ready, you would be let out to play. When the weather was fine we would play in the grounds but until you reached your teens you were never allowed outside the grounds unescorted, except for going to school. On Saturday afternoons we were taken to the local sweetshop and off to the nearby hills for walks. In the summer months when it was fine we would take a picnic and stop on the Malvern Hills (which are also known as the Worcestershire Beacons) till about 6.00 in the evening. The time spent on these hills was exciting in many ways, and my favourite pastime once we settled at the top was to sit and daydream. You could see for miles whichever direction you faced and I always wondered what was beyond the horizon. None of my daydreams came true.

Every Sunday we would have the usual early morning routine until after breakfast. All the lads then attended the 10.00 am church service at St Peter's Church followed by Sunday School in the afternoons. In my last few years at St Peter's I had the privilege of serving as an altar boy.

I always loved church music, and just the church itself. Going into church, whether or not there was a service taking place, gave me a wonderful feeling of serene peace, although ironically I was to be denied this comfort later in life.

Each summer everyone went to a seaside resort. We usually stayed in the local children's home or a hall, but on one occasion most of us were taken in by local families. This made a wonderful change, and we were very grateful to the people who showed us great kindness. I shall never forget that week of delight and I have fond memories of being taken to the beach and being given some freshly-smoked kippers: I have never tasted kippers like it before or since. I couldn't put into words the happiness and insight into family life this holiday gave me, but afterwards I felt so low and so desperate to belong that I never accepted another offer to stay in someone else's home.

* * *

At Christmas time we would have at least three parties as well as outings to pantomimes. We always had plenty of toys and games too, even in 1947 when the country was going through its worst winter for years. Being in an orphanage had its advantages: I don't suppose for one minute that the local people, especially the kids, had the parties, toys, outings and holidays we had, so in some ways we were far better off. However, the first day back at school after the Christmas holidays always made me feel so different. The other boys and girls would be chattering away saying 'My father did this . . .' or 'My mother said that . . .' or 'My brother, sister and I . . .'. Although I was educationally backward I never missed much that went on around me, and it was innocent everyday remarks like these that made me yearn all the more to belong. As I grew older this feeling grew, and it was to play an important part in my later life.

* * *

When I was coming up to my ninth birthday, something happened that had an effect on me for years afterwards. Since the night when I was frightened by the cockroaches I'd been terrified of the dark but I could cope with late winter afternoons until one afternoon when I was coming back from school on my own. I took the short-cut through the churchyard and as I reached the vicarage I was accosted by a tramp who frightened me so much I couldn't speak. The next morning I woke up while it was still dark and had my first asthma attack. My asthma is mainly psychosomatic but the symptoms are very real and it gets worse at times of deep fear and loneliness.

* * *

On 4 February 1953, when I was 11, I was sent to Rydd Court School for educationally backward children. I enjoyed the long car ride to the school, which was near Upton-on-Severn, and hardly noticed the pouring rain.

Rydd Court is set just off the Malvern/Worcestershire road, and used to be a military officers' hospital. We drove through a thick net of woods on either side of the gravel driveway which opened into the grounds, and drew up to an enormous building. The huge grounds were immaculate, and you wouldn't have believed it possible for a place like this to exist in such a wilderness.

Entering the main hall, the first person I saw was the caretaker who was about six foot tall and very broad with quite a long beard. I didn't want to stay when the Master went, but once I got over the first few days I settled down and the change in me was quite something.

My new number was 14, and I was placed in the green school line. There were four houses: blue, red, green and yellow. I was in green, which meant that whenever assembly was called I would line up in the green line. Each house had a leader and a deputy who was responsible for assemblies and in charge of his colour's dormitory area. I became a deputy colour leader twice and was disgraced twice.

After a few days I wanted to write a letter to the Master but couldn't as I was unable to read or write. This gave me the incentive I needed and I was determined to learn. Thereafter I started to tackle the basic three Rs with the help of the teachers who were very understanding.

The school was run by Mr and Mrs Long who lived on the top floor. They were very good to me in general ways and gave me far more rope than some would have. The other teachers, Miss Killon, Mr Peters, Mr Jones and Mr Evans were all good teachers and an asset to the school. Miss Killon tried hard to teach me to play the piano, but as much as I loved music, I wasn't cut out to be a pianist. My first love was maths, but I found spelling difficult simply because I had problems with my speech. Even now I'm unable to pronounce quite a few words which is why my spelling is still atrocious.

Classes at Rydd Court varied from the basic three Rs to nature and mechanics. The mechanics class was held in the evenings and it was very practical. One project was to strip down an old van and rebuild it into an open training van. This took months to do and when it was finished we were taught to drive. Mr Jones was always finding projects such as this which would be beneficial to us.

Sportswise Rydd Court was equally good: we learned hockey, tennis, swimming, cricket, football and boxing. I only tried boxing once, broke my hand and never tried it again! In fact I broke my right arm three times within 18 months which is how I became left-handed. I loved football, but I had two left feet and wasn't picked to play very often. I lost quite a bit of my confidence on the hockey pitch after I was hit on the side of the head by a hockey ball, although I never stopped enjoying the game. Cricket bored me until later in life. Learning to swim was easy: I fell in at the deep end of the pool and nearly drowned which made me determined to learn properly.

We had evening activities such as chess, draughts, music and drama, and on Thursday evenings there was a film show. Routine at the school varied a lot and I enjoyed living in. To me it was the perfect home and school in one, and in fact I enjoyed it so much that the rest of the world seemed to pass unnoticed until the end of each term.

★   ★   ★

While I was at Rydd Court I discovered a side of me that was to cause many problems and a great deal of pain for a good part of my life. We were allowed to watch television from 5.30 until 8.00 pm in the winter months, and one evening I noticed two brothers kissing. I told my friend Philip about it and wondered if he'd seen it too. He said he had and that there was nothing wrong in it, and promised to give me a goodnight kiss when we went to bed. At that moment something stirred inside me: I didn't understand it and didn't try to; I just knew I was looking forward to bedtime. Philip and I had been friends since our arrival at Rydd Court, and although we spent a lot of time together nothing like this had come into our friendship before. I was 13 and I suppose this was the first homosexual act I had committed, although I'd been aware of feeling 'different'

6

about one or two boys since the age of 11.

I returned to St Peter's Home for the summer and Christmas holidays but I always felt the odd one out. There were always new boys and as I was only around for a few weeks in the holidays I didn't have time to fit in with any of the groups of friends. However I did get friendly with the odd lad. It was during one of the four week Christmas breaks that I met Frankie. He was two years younger than me and how I envied him. He was bright and intelligent, and seemed to be able to make friends easily. Whenever I came back to the home he always found time for me and I enjoyed his company. Despite his friendship however I sometimes got very low and would sit in my corner on the radiator and cry without shame, just as I did when I first went to St Peter's. I suppose in a way I was my own worst enemy because I didn't try to help myself when I felt low.

★ ★ ★

Looking back on my days at St Peter's Home I remember an awful lot of good times which must outweigh the lonely periods, but I think that two major incidents I've never forgotten have had long-term effects. I was told I was going to be adopted at one stage, but because I was at Rydd Court the couple decided it would be ill-advised. The second and more important incident was a heart-breaking one. The Master died while I was away at Rydd Court and the news was broken to me by a boy who made a big joke of it. When I was told officially that it was no joke, the Master *was* gone, I went mad. Had it not been for the fact that I would pass out as soon as I saw blood, God knows what I might have done to the boy who told me in such a cruel way. After I left school I would visit the Master's grave as often as possible without letting anyone know, for I found great comfort in having thought of him as my secret father.

Mrs Mullock carried on at St Peter's for a while and then left to run a children's home in Ledbury with Joyce and Roll Trany. In 1959 she was the subject of *This is Your Life.*

After she left, going back to the home for holidays was never the same and by the age of 14 I had become very unsettled at school as well. My behaviour, whilst not outrageous, was far from good, and my learning suffered. I started asking about my mother, because I dearly wanted to know what my family was like, and I formed a special friendship with Ian. I so much needed to belong, and it was not too long before I came to love him. I would do anything for him, although I knew he didn't feel the same towards me. I suppose we had sex, if you could call it that; we used to kiss and cuddle, and occasionally masturbated each other. Some nights I used to sleep in his bed — although we were in different dormitories I was a deputy colour leader and could go into his room without anyone questioning it. Each night a different member of staff slept in on night duty, and one night Ian and I were caught together. I lost my colour leader post (quite rightly) and got the slipper — how the teacher could use that slipper! Next morning I was disgraced in front of the school, and Ian would have nothing to do with me for months afterwards, but that didn't stop my feelings for him.

★ ★ ★

Just before we went on Christmas leave each year we put on our own pantomime in the hall where we held church services, music classes and gym and games sessions. One particular year we performed *The Singing Policeman.* I was chosen to play the policeman, singing to woo his loved one, and for this part I had to wear a real policeman's uniform. One of the teachers took me to Malvern police station to borrow an old uniform.

It was strange that I should be chosen for this part since I'd wanted to be a policeman from the early age of eight. I'd admired the local policeman who came to St Peter's Home to collect the swill for his pigs. He was a big ginger-haired man who always found time to stop for a chat with us lads.

I was really looking forward to the show, but I was never to perform. One morning a week before the dress rehearsal and performance I got up and went out like a light; every time I got up the same thing happened. I didn't know what day or even what week it was until I was woken up in the sickbay and saw the whole cast of the show, including another lad in my policeman's uniform. It really upset me, although it was done with the best intentions.

That Christmas was the first without Mr Mullock, and while I was well looked after, as usual, I was unsettled and was pleased to get back to school where I felt more at home.

★　★　★

The last year or so at Rydd Court seemed an unreal time. I knew I would have to leave the school and home I had come to rely on, probably too much, but I had no idea where to go, or what to do, or what to expect. I had never been further than the seaside on holidays, and had only visited the local shops and the nearby town a few times. Through television programmes like the nightly news I had gained some idea of what went on in the outside world, but I didn't like the thought of leaving school, and as the time drew near I became more and more unsettled. My behaviour must have caused some concern both at Rydd Court and at St Peter's Home, and I wonder now if I had become institutionalised at this early age.

The time came to leave Rydd Court when I was 16. I had to face reality and accept that I wouldn't be going back to school after the Christmas holidays, and I felt so low and afraid. Mr Long took me from Rydd Court to St Peter's Home and I tried to thank him for all he and his staff had done but no words seemed to come. We shook hands and that was the last I was to see of him although I did visit the school again. I went back for the next yearly open day and I wished I hadn't. You can't go back, only forward.

NINE MONTHS IN SOCIETY

On leaving school I owned £5.00 worth of premium bonds, which I had saved for out of my nine pence a week pocket money, and the clothing I stood up in, which was given to me by the school. The home kitted me out with all the clothing I would need to start my working life.

As I had left school officially I should have left the home after the Christmas holidays, but finding me a job and lodgings was proving to be somewhat difficult for the welfare officer who was responsible for me until I reached the age of 18. I tried the army and several jobs without much success, so I was allowed to stay on at St Peter's for a while.

Mr and Mrs Sherman had taken over at St Peter's shortly before I left school. They were a young couple and although they ran the home in a totally different way from Mr and Mrs Mullock, they cared for us with just as much understanding. The Shermans showed me great kindness throughout this difficult time and long after I had found a job and left St Peter's. I think it must be a special kind of person who takes on this demanding work.

The welfare officer wasn't having any luck, so I decided to look for work on my own, and found a part-time job through an advertisement in a local shop window. I earned five shillings doing odd jobs for two elderly ladies four evenings a week.

How I finally found my first full-time job was quite odd. The local YMCA boss Mr Cooper was coming to look round St Peter's. On this particular day Mr and Mrs Sherman were short of staff and had other visitors, so I was asked to look after Mr Cooper. Before he arrived I put my best suit on and decided what might interest him in St Peter's. While we were going round the home, we got talking about whether I was working and what I would like to do. I told him I wanted to become a policeman, but as I was too young as yet I was willing to try any kind of work. At the end of the visit he invited me to have a look round the YMCA, and while on this visit he offered me the job of relief porter. I accepted with a sense of pride and excitement.

Mr and Mrs Sherman arranged with the welfare officer that I could stay on at St Peter's to begin with as I was to work 9.00 till 5.00, Monday to Friday, and this wouldn't interfere with the home's routine. It also meant that I could continue with my jobs for the two elderly ladies. As I was earning a wage I did this unpaid, but was given supper and had a chat with the ladies after I finished the jobs. My new job and times meant I also continued going to church and serving at the altar. Had I had to move at the beginning, I don't know if I would have settled into the YMCA job so well.

I continued like this for about three months and then moved into the YMCA. As a relief porter I was required to cover any shift or job, and on any day I might be a kitchen porter, gardener (a job I grew to dislike), storeman or handyman. I also relieved staff in YMCAs in other parts of the country. My place of work was next to the Winter Gardens, Malvern. The theatre, picture house and swimming pool were less than two minutes away, so I didn't have far to wander. The only time I would go further afield was to visit St Peter's or go to church, and that would only take place during the daylight hours. I spent most of my off-duty time at the pictures, swimming, watching television, or playing records. Everything was going well and I was enjoying life, but what was to come in such a short time I could not have foreseen.

My first mistake was to see the Hitchcock film *The Birds* which frightened me so much that I ran screaming from the picture house and went back to my room. I was too terrified to stay there so I went to the nearest public house for company. I started drinking beer, which I wasn't used to, and the next thing I knew I was in the local police station. Luckily the sergeant-in-charge knew me. An inspector gave me a dressing down, and I was taken back to the YMCA in a police car. This didn't go down well with my boss, and very soon it seemed as if I could do nothing right. I spent most of my time in the stores where Mr Cooper's wife worked, and he began to think there was something between us, which created a bad atmosphere.

As luck would have it, I was transferred to a YMCA in Darlington on relief duties, but I soon put my foot in it there too. I had been at Darlington YMCA for just over a month and had made friends with two Londoners who worked there. They bet me that I couldn't insert a hypodermic needle into my arm like they had done. I did, and won the £5.00 bet. To this day I'm still not sure what was in the needle. Whatever it was, it had no effect on them, but to be on the safe side I went to my local GP. He reported me to my new boss, who in turn contacted my welfare officer. She arranged for the YMCA to transfer me back to Malvern. I felt that the matter had been blown up out of all proportion.

Back on duty at Malvern one evening, I was going from the kitchen to the small television lounge when I smelt burning and seconds later saw smoke coming up the stairway. Very quickly I rang for the fire brigade and set off the alarms. The fire was put out before too much damage had been done, and I was interviewed by the police and the chief fire officer since I had made the phone call and set off the alarms. As far as I was concerned I had done everything right, but next morning my boss gave me the impression that he thought *I* had started the fire. What can you do in such a situation apart from treating the accusation with the contempt it deserves?

A couple of days later my welfare officer came on the scene and the next thing I knew I was interviewed by a Dr Grant. I was given the alternative of either going into Powick, the local mental hospital, for assessment as a voluntary patient, or being committed by a doctor. I went in as a voluntary patient, and within a few weeks was informed that I could leave. I went back to my job but in less than a fortnight I had a difference of opinion with Mr Cooper and found myself out of a job — and my home. I was too old to go back to St Peter's and had nowhere else to go, so the welfare officer advised me to return to Powick, promising me I would be able to find a new job and lodgings from there.

I had lasted nine months in society. I may have acted foolishly at times, but what was happening to me wasn't called for. Little did I know it was just the beginning of a nightmare that would last for many years.

POWICK

When I first returned to Powick I enjoyed an easy life playing cards and tennis, walking, and going to the weekly picture shows. There was a dance every Wednesday evening, and a nurse taught me to dance. In fact all the staff were very good to me.

I felt I was in a false world and a part of me wanted to go back into the world I had known for only a short time, but on the other hand I felt safer and more secure within this environment. Mr Jones, one of the teachers from Rydd Court, came to see me and for the first time in a long while I was able to talk to someone I trusted and respected. At the end of the visit I asked him not to come again because I felt I had let him down by ending up in Powick. I didn't wander far outside the hospital, apart from the odd trip to the shops, so there was little chance of coming into contact with anyone else from the home or school.

I was begining to enjoy being with the opposite sex at dances, bingo and card sessions, until one evening when I was on my way to collect the ward's tea. A female patient got hold of me and frightened me so much that I ran back to the ward and forgot about the tea. She wanted to kiss me and do things that reminded me of the time I was stopped by the tramp. I didn't go off the ward on my own for ages after that, nor have anything to do with women. I even stopped dancing with the nurse.

*   *   *

I bought a sharp knife just after going into Powick the second time. I had so much time on my hands and would spend hours in the woods where the knife came in very handy. My first mistake was lending it to a friend of mine. The next thing I found out was that Billy had been committed to hospital under a court order, but was planning to run off. I asked him to give me my knife back as I knew that if he got into trouble with it my chances of joining the police force would be nil — I stood very little chance anyway as things now stood. I confronted him in the driveway and was standing there with the knife in my hand when a doctor saw us. Nothing was said to either of us, but two staff members were called to escort me back to the ward and I was kept in for three days. No-one apart from the charge nurse on the ward asked me about the incident, although I would have thought that some explanation would be expected.

My relationship with Billy was just like any other teenage friendship. However my friendship with Jim was a mixed affair to say the least. We were the same age but worlds apart in that Jim was

11

a lot brighter than I and nobody's fool. He was very crafty and didn't have the same sense of honesty and respect for authority I had. We formed a relationship, but it proved in time to be the first of the one-sided relationships that were to cause deep internal conflict between my need to belong and to love another person and my respect for the law and the church. By no means am I a religious person, but someone who has been brought up in the teachings of the Church of England Children's Society does not easily foresake his way of life.

When Jim told me he was going to London to join a pick-pocket gang, I decided to go along with him. I hoped to find out as much as I could and then inform the police, hence putting me on a better footing when I applied to join the force. We travelled to London and went to a cinema just off Leicester Square. About ten minutes after we arrived Jim said he was going to the toilet and asked me to look out for the contact. Fifteen minutes later I realised that I didn't even know what sort of contact I was supposed to be looking for, so I went to find Jim. He had gone. I felt a real clot, and decided to see if he was waiting somewhere outside the cinema. London being London, it wasn't long before I was completely lost.

After three days I decided enough was enough. I walked up to the nearest policeman and told him I was lost, explaining who I was and why I was there. He took me to the nearest police station where I was well looked after until the next morning when Mr Stevenson, a welfare officer from the Church of England Children's Society, came to escort me back to Powick by train. We had a long talk, and got to know each other quite well. His job was just to take me back to Powick, but his interest in me didn't end there. For as long as I needed his friendship and help, even at times when I rejected him, he never lost interest in me. Mr Stevenson was to go to a lot of trouble to help me find my mother.

Jim returned to Powick a week or so after I did, but I never did ask him what happened in London. We remained friends and spent a lot of time together, the only thing I disliked about him being his attitude towards crime. One Wednesday night we decided to give the weekly whistdrive a miss. It was a sunny evening and just right for a walk. We finished up lying together in a field, and it was the first time Jim and I really let ourselves go. At this time I thought I knew a lot, but little did I realise I still had a lot to learn.

On the walk back Jim got on to the subject of murder. I was determined to frighten him out of this stupidity, so I put my hand over his mouth. I scared him, as I had intended to. That evening back on the ward most of us were sitting around talking about medical matters, and just to be on the safe side after hearing this conversation I told the charge nurse how I had scared Jim. The next morning I was seen by Dr Grant and then transferred to the block, the only locked wards in Powick.

Some time later I was interviewed by five people. I wasn't introduced to them or even told who they were, although I knew Dr Grant and Dr Edwards, who had visited St Peter's. They asked me what my ambition was. I replied that I wanted to be a policeman. Then they asked if I would kill a policeman. I thought this was a stupid question, considering my first answer, and gave what I thought was a suitably stupid reply. Yes, I *would* kill a policeman.

Later that week I was asked if I would like to be transferred to a different hospital where they could help me. I said I would if it was in my best interests: little did I know I had no choice in the matter.

On 1 October 1959 I was on my way to East Retford in Nottinghamshire to the other hospital. I was told it was called Rampton and that it was a good place. Never having heard of Rampton before, I looked forward to getting there.

2. RAMPTON 1959-65

'This Rampton . . . you don't answer back and you don't question anything you see'

FIRST IMPRESSIONS

The nearer I got to Rampton Hospital, which is also known as the Broadmoor of the North, the bigger it seemed to grow. I stepped out of the car into the warm sun, and walked up the three steps leading to the main entrance. The two nurses who had brought me from Powick took me into a small sitting room, and it was not long before a middle-aged man in a grey coat came to collect me. As I went to pick up my case the man, who I later found out to be an occupation officer, said 'I'll carry that for you, Mr Harding'. I said goodbye to the two nurses and they said they hoped it wouldn't be too long before I went back to Powick. At this stage I didn't realise what was in store for me.

As we came to a door I noticed that my escort opened it with a big key and that the window near the door had thick bars painted white. It reminded me of the Frankie Vaughan song *What's behind the green door?* Just through the door was a big yard with locked doors leading to different places. There were bars on all the windows. I thought this must be the equivalent to the annexes in Powick. I'd arrived at about 1.15 pm, so there was little movement on the long dark cream and green corridor. The first person we met was a man wearing a blue uniform; I glanced at the person I was with and noticed he had the same sort of uniform on under his grey coat. I asked who had just passed us, and he gave me the information for which I have been grateful ever since: 'This is Rampton and all persons you see here in uniform or in grey or green overalls you call Sir. You don't answer back at any time and you don't question anything you see. Don't make any close friends among your fellow patients if you want to have an easy ride and get out some time'.

By the time I got to the admission ward, Eden — usually known as El, I was dumbfounded. I knew nothing about Rampton, yet if I had read what my escort had told me correctly, I would have to see nothing, hear nothing and say nothing if I wanted to get out.

While walking along Eden corridor I was told to keep off the redwork which ran along each side of the corridor like a plate of glass. Outside the ward office I was told to stop and stand up straight. The person escorting me had changed his attitude by now, and I soon found out that this was common practice. Some staff, when on their own with you, would treat you quite sympathetically but change their tune as soon as other staff were around simply because of the military way in which Rampton was run. Within a few seconds I was taken into a bathroom next door to the office and told to strip off and get into the bath. Five big members of staff stood watching me. I was about to say something but had second thoughts after the reaction of my escort into El. Thank God I did. After the bath I had to put on a hospital nightshirt, and I never saw my own clothing after that.

I caught my first glimpse of my fellow inmates as I was escorted down a corridor which led

14

through to two rooms in which a lot of them were playing cards. The first patient I was to speak to was Ted, an elderly man who was obviously in a trusted position. He brought my meals into my room, and always had a pleasant word to say although he didn't know anything about me. This was common as no patient was allowed to know why another patient was in Rampton. However you could tell a lot about a patient by the sort of unofficial interview he got.

There are two kinds of interview in Rampton. One is an official interview where the member of staff talks to you in an office or a private room. With the other sort of interview, anything goes as long as the patient can't prove to anyone in authority that he's been beaten up. 'Unofficial' interviews can happen anywhere, and Queensberry rules do not apply. I was informed by the charge nurse on E1 that I could have an easy or hard ride at Rampton, and that Rampton had tamed lions.

My first official interview was with Dr Richardson who at this stage of his career was a medical officer. After the routine medical, which all new patients have, we sat talking for two hours about religious matters. I found Dr Richardson to be very sincere about this subject. He made me feel as though there was some future for me and that I still belonged to the human race and, what was more important, that God hadn't forsaken me.

After the interview with Dr Richardson I was put in a small locked room with just a bed and a gentleman's pot. There was a big shutter over the window. After a couple of hours I started to wonder what I had done by allowing myself to be transferred to this. I decided that it could only get better and that I must give it a try. If I didn't like it, I would discharge myself. (I was still not aware that I had been admitted to Rampton under the Mental Health Act and had no right to leave without permission.)

Then I had my first hair cut, if you could call it that. A small basin was put over the top of my head and any hair showing was cut off. The basin was then taken off and the rest of the hair trimmed. I had awful hair so I didn't mind this too much at the time.

*　　*　　*

Three days had gone by and the only time I had been allowed out of my room was to go to the clinic for a blood test and to have white stuff put around my private parts, which was very painful. On the fourth morning I was issued with one pair of socks, one set of underwear, one shirt, one tie, one pair of braces, one pair of slippers, one pair of shoes, one working suit, one best suit, one handkerchief, one pair of overalls, one toothbrush, one piece of soap, one hand towel, one overcoat and one locker key. I was informed that should I damage or lose any of this hospital property I would be sent to Drake Ward — D1. This was the first I was to hear of the infamous D1, but by no means the last.

My best suit was taken away by the ward storeman. I changed into hospital clothing, and put the rest of the things I'd been issued into my locker. My locker number was the same as my ward number — number 12. I was then set to work decking the office corridor. A decker is a small weighted brush attached to a pole six or seven feet long. It's very awkward to handle until you've spent months working with it, and if you're not careful you can easily hurt yourself or anyone else who happens to be in the way.

At dinner I met the rest of my fellow inmates on E1 for the first time. Some wanted to know me, some didn't. The food was surprisingly good, although I drew the line at finding a sanitary towel in the tea. After that I stuck to drinking water straight from the tap.

On my fourth day at Rampton I also met Mr Stewart, the chief male nurse. Right from the start I got the impression that this man was good and fair, and my first impression in time proved correct. He took me into the office and asked me a few questions about some people at Powick, and then told me that if I behaved myself he would see that I was dealt with fairly. I was to find out that his word was his bond, a quality I have always believed to be important. On the same day I received an internal letter setting out Rampton's rules and regulations. Dr Murray was to be my responsible medical officer, and if I wished to discuss anything to do with my treatment or discharge from Rampton, I should refer the matter to him. I could apply to see an officer from the Ministry of Health by writing for an interview. I was allowed one free letter a week, and I would receive pocket money once a month. My hospital number was to be 3021 and I should use this number when making any official request. Even at this stage it didn't sink in that I was in Rampton under Section 60 of the Mental Health Act 1959, otherwise known as a hospital order.

I made some mistakes that first day on the ward, like mislaying my key, and was given extra work as a punishment. By 6.30 pm it was time to go to bed, with lights out at 7.30 — it was horrible. It didn't go down well with me at all, but I had enough sense not to complain. Trying to sleep for 11½ hours out of 24 was all right for the first few days in Rampton because of the pressure you were under, but after that it was no joke.

WARD E1

The daily routine on E1 in 1959 was as follows: up at 7.00 pm, strip bed for inspection, then make a Rampton bedpack. This meant folding your blanket and sheets into a square, then putting your pillow and pillowcases into your counterpane which would have to be folded the same size as the blankets and sheets and laid centrally on the bed. Then we would collect our clothing from the storeman, undress and change in the corridor looking out onto the villa area, go to be shaved by one of the staff, wash, and start our jobs. My first job on E1 was sweeping and decking the office corridor and I was later moved to scrubbing out the toilets. This was a blessing in that I could at least go to the toilet when I wanted.

Breakfast was at 7.45 for an hour, then it was work again. 10.15 tea break in the cloakroom, then work until 11.30 with dinner at 12 noon. New patients then went back to work at 1.30 until 4.30, and people who had been there three weeks could go outside from 2.30 until 4.15. 4.45 tea, 5.15 work, 6.00 change for bed, 6.30 bed, 7.30 lights out.

The reason for such a tight routine was that E1 was the breaking-in ward; as a new patient you were an unknown quantity, so the staff had to sort out what kind of person you were. Staff went through a breaking-in routine too, and it was just as bad for them. Novice members of staff would have no keys and would be put on duty in the sick corridor under the supervision of a senior staff nurse. In their first week at Rampton they would be shown how to use the boot without hurting the foot, and would be put in a situation where they would be expected to use boot force. If a novice refused to play along, staff would make his life difficult until he either conformed or resigned. I know of one novice who stated that he had become a nurse to help make patients better, not to mistreat them. He didn't last long at Rampton.

                  *   *   *

One morning not long after I arrived on E1, I was told to put my best suit on. I began to wonder what was going on, but it didn't take long to find out. I was taken to see Dr Rolands, a soft-spoken man who at this time was the medical superintendent. I put my trust in him straightaway, and was never to have cause to doubt his sincerity and concern for the patients' well-being, although we were to have our differences in later years.

                  *   *   *

A few weeks later I had my first encounter with bumming. I call it 'bumming' rather than a homosexual act because I believe that if two people have sex as an expression of their affection for one another, that is an act of loving.

On this occasion, however, the storeman wanted to have intercourse with me to satisfy his own desires and was prepared to force me into it by stating that he would make life difficult for me. To me that is bumming, and if a man and a woman have sex for money, it amounts to the same thing. I was not prepared to submit to blackmail, so I went to the office and asked the charge nurse for a transfer to a different ward. When asked why I wanted to move, I said I was not prepared to state my reason as it was my word against that of another patient without proof. I decided on this course of action as I knew what would happen to the other person if I gave my reasons. The charge nurse asked me to tell him what had happened without revealing the other person's name. I did, and he promptly told me the name of the other person concerned. I had learned another lesson the hard way. However I was transferred to E3 (Evans Ward), and the storeman was not sent to D1 as I had feared he might be. By this time I knew what D1 was like, and had promised myself that I would never get anyone into trouble if it could be avoided.

WARD E3

At Rampton all new patients start off on E1. Where they go next depends on their age and which section of the Mental Health Act they're on. C3 is for severely mentally handicapped people, C2 is for patients who don't fit into any of the other categories at Rampton, C1 is an empty ward which can be used when other wards are being painted. D3 is for eps (epileptic patients), D2 is for top security patients, D1 is supposed to be for anyone and everyone who is in Rampton because they've committed a crime or are mentally ill, yet it's also the punishment ward. E2 is for patients who are over 21, E3 for patients between the ages of 14 to 21 and Moss House is the children's ward. Yes, I was as shocked as you must be that at this time there were children from the age of six upwards living in a God-forsaken place like Rampton.

A change of ward meant a change of daily routine. After breakfast on E3, we collected our overalls and then waited in the cloakrooms until a shop boss, as they were called, came and collected us for the occupational shops where we worked from 9.00 till 11.30, and again from 1.00 till 4.30. After about two weeks on E3 I was interviewed by Mr Brooks, the chief occupation officer. He asked me what my ambition was and I told him the same as I had told everyone else, so he decided that I should be allocated to E working shop. I was given a car engine to strip and clean, and found this job very interesting. It took me some months to finish, and in any case I was in no hurry to get it done as it gave me something to look forward to. One had precious little else to look forward to in Rampton. Most patients enjoyed the time they spent in the occupational shops as the staff there were very different from those on the ward: they gave you more room to be yourself and earned your respect rather than demanding it.

After tea, which was at 4.45 (only once in a blue moon did the time vary), the patients on the buckshee table would clean the ward for half an hour. A different set of patients were on the buckshee table every day, and most people looked forward to their turn as it meant extra food. After tea we could do what we liked until bedtime at 7.00. We were always stopped and searched before we were allowed into the dormitories or side rooms: it was awful and I never did get used to it.

*   *   *

Mr Stewart — or Bert, to use his nickname — visited every ward once a day. He knew every patient by name, and had a nickname for most of them — mine was Bonehead. Although he had his favourites, Bert was as fair as the day was long, and he didn't let staff get away with anything. I remember once on E3 Bert told a staff nurse to get his hair cut and even gave him half a crown to do so, as long as he got the money back on pay day. On another occasion, a staff nurse was smoking on the ward, which was forbidden. When Bert came through the door, the nurse hid the cigarette behind his back, so Bert stood talking to him until he burned his hand. Mr Stewart was nobody's fool, and at this time he ran Rampton.

* * *

Dr Rolands took over from Dr O'Malley in 1958. He had previously been Dr O'Malley's deputy, but had no real power and had to accept the system at Rampton for what it was. After he took over he decided to implement his own ideas. From what I can gather, Rampton was at least 30 years behind the times when Dr Rolands took over, so when I arrived in 1959, the hospital was going through a honeymoon period.

Changes in Rampton were bound to be slow and hard to achieve for two major reasons. Apart from Dr Rolands, most of the officials had been there since God knows when. It was like a tight-knit family business with two generations of many families working there, so if you offended one person you often offended a dozen without knowing it. The only qualifications staff needed were that they were over 18 and well-built, and had served in the forces.

The other reason why changes would inevitably be slow to happen was that responsibility for running Rampton had just been transferred from the Home Office to the Ministry of Health (now the Department of Health and Social Security), so the admin side was still unsettled.

* * *

Just before Christmas 1959 I wrote to Dr Murray about my release and he arranged to see me in his office (at this time doctors never went onto the wards to interview their patients). It was at this meeting that I found out I was in Rampton under a hospital order. The hospital order had been enforced because I had attacked a patient with a knife, joined a pick-pocket gang, and attempted to suffocate a patient. I was classified as subnormal. I'd been denied the basic human right of knowing what I was accused of. I couldn't understand how this could have happened; all I wanted in life was to be a policeman. It upset me so much I was depressed for days: all I could do was cry and ask myself why. I'm no angel; I acted foolishly, even stupidly, but I was no criminal.

Christmas came and went, thank God.

ESCAPE?

It didn't take me long to start thinking of ways to escape. Most of us used to spend hours working out escape schemes, but although a lot of plans were made, very few were carried out because of the price you had to pay if caught. The penalty for escaping from Rampton was D1.

I'd already had my first taste of D1 by this time. At weekends or shop holiday times, some patients would be taken from the block wards to scrub the main corridors, and we had to get our equipment from D1. On one occasion I was told to scrub the floors on D1, and while I was doing this a fellow patient was brought in. Some staff went into the side rooms and the one in charge of the cleaning party told us to stop what we were doing and move around to the other corridor. Later I noticed that the window of the door to the side room where staff had taken the patient was painted white. You didn't need a particularly vivid imagination to guess what had gone on behind closed doors.

If a patient is escorted into D1 by police or outsiders, he walks; if not, his feet don't touch the ground until he's in number 2 or 5 side room. He's then put into a canvas suit which has sleeves that can be tied behind his back, and locked in the side room with just a mattress, blanket and sheets. There he stays for 28 days with a minimum of food and drink and plenty of unofficial interviews. At the end of the 28 days he's put on 14 to 21 days punishment which means from the moment he gets up until the moment he goes to bed, except for short mealtimes, he scrubs the corridors and side rooms. A patient's length of stay on D1 depends on what he's done; I heard of one person who did 15 years there for trying to escape.

Getting out of Rampton was very much on my mind when I walked into E3 quiet room one day and stumbled upon a final get-together for a few lads who were going to escape. They obviously thought I had heard more than I had. I was invited to go along and agreed, but I soon changed my mind when I was informed of their full plan. Although I was prepared to go — and damn good luck to anyone else who wanted to go — I couldn't condone a plan which involved guns and stealing. By all means take a chance of escaping by trickery and breaking the rules, and steal food of the land to survive, but violence is just not on. My change of heart caused a lot of ill-feeling until I assured them that I wouldn't shop them, but it came to the point where I had little choice. One of the group, Nick, decided that the risk of taking a chance on me was too great and that I would have to be dealt with. This meant that they would get me into trouble so that I would be sent to D1, but another member of the group whom I was having a bit of an affair with told me what was going on. I decided that if I was to go to D1, I would go for a good reason, so I offered to pay another lad to keep Nick off my back, knowing full well that the lad, Dave, was a shopper (a person who tells the staff what's going on). Dave went into the office, as I'd predicted he would, and of course I was called in to explain why I'd paid him. I told the charge nurse that I'd set Dave up to get at Nick who was going to trick me because he disliked me and felt I was getting too big for my boots. Nick was then called in and he really put his foot in it. The charge nurse sent for Mr Stewart, but there was no proof that a big move was about to be made. Nick and I got extra work and nothing more. The escape never took place, and nobody got hurt, thank God, so it worked out quite well for all concerned.

My golden opportunity to escape came along in June 1960. After each meal the can lads (the most junior members of staff on the ward) would escort the three patients whose job was to take the empty food containers back to the kitchen and then empty the swill and paper bins just outside the big green gates. Somehow the can lad mis-escorted and I missed going back through the gate. When I realised I was on my own, my first reaction was to knock on the green gate, but then it dawned on me that a golden opportunity had presented itself. I waited to see if anyone had heard my knock on the green gate. No-one had, and by this time the can lad must have arrived back on the ward without realising he was one down. I knew I had at least half an hour before I would be missed.

I was wearing hospital clothing which would make me stick out like a sore thumb if I started running, so I decided to walk. I reckoned that if I walked any staff who saw me would think I was out on a job. My luck ran out a few yards from the green gate. Mr Jamieson, one of the staff from C shop, came down the road leading to the front entrance, stopped me and asked me what I was doing. I told him I had been locked out and was trying to find a way to get back in as I couldn't draw anyone's attention at the gate. I was scared stiff and the truth must have been written all over my face. However, Mr Jamieson took me through the big green gates and told me to go and bang on the window of E1 until someone let me in. He also told me that he wouldn't say he'd found me waiting outside the door. I could never repay this debt as he could quite easily have taken me to D1 for attempting to go absent without leave, which is the official term for being on the run.

Bert came to see me that evening and asked me a few questions about the incident. The poor can lad got a right telling off, but it was his own fault and I was rather pleased to have got away with it.

CAUGHT IN THE SYSTEM

Being on E3 was proving to be a horrible experience. The dormitory was far too small for the number of people in it, and E3 was known throughout the hospital as the trainee jockey club — and, believe me, sexual activity didn't only take place between the patients.

I was beginning to lower my standards although I really didn't fit in with the inner crowd on E3, which made life even more lonely. I was going through a stage where I was surrounded by people, yet I felt alone and needed so much to belong. Mr Stevenson was doing all he could to try to find my mother, but without success.

One day a welfare officer brought Micky, my friend from St Peter's, to see me. He had started to look for his mother at the same time as me, and I was very pleased to learn he had found her. They were living together as a family, and getting on well. It was so nice to see Micky — I never knew how much a visit by a close friend meant. Micky looked so well and so contented with life, and I was overwhelmed to think he had taken so much time and trouble to come all the way from Somerset to see me.

Back on E3, I was happy that I had seen my friend, but as the evening went by I felt lower and lower. I got under my bedclothes and cried like I used to at St Peter's, but here I couldn't call out for the Master. My secret dad had died, and how I wished that God would take me too.

Days, weeks, passed by. Through my own weakness I had succumbed to the Rampton system and was becoming institutionalised. Not caring, not knowing and unable to see any light. I lived in a make-believe world, and had it not been for Derek starting to bite his fingers off, and George going out of his mind, God knows what might have happened. I could have easily ended up the same way, but these two people's misfortunes gave me the shock I needed to pull myself together. The worst part about becoming institutionalised is that you don't realise it is happening. Only other people, like staff and patients who are in day-to-day contact with you, can tell there's something wrong.

I decided I needed a hobby to give me an interest in the outside world and to keep me occupied in my spare time. Mr Redman, a junior staff nurse, suggested I take up stamp collecting as he'd had many hours' enjoyment from this hobby himself. When he was on the 2.00 till 7.00 shift he would always spend as much time as he could with the lads, and he gave me a lot of help with my stamp collection.

Things were better for a while, but soon time began to have no meaning again. I needed something more than my stamps — I needed to feel I belonged. There was no news about my mother, I had no close friends, and even in the overcrowded day room I felt alone, so I started getting involved in internal politics. I found out that for staff and patients alike the only way to survive was to get to know the right people, to be two-faced and to use the system. I was at a disadvantage, however, in that my word has always been my bond. Mr Mullock told me that no matter what happened in life, as long as you kept your promises people would accept and respect you. Therefore I could tell white lies, but when I gave my word on matters of importance, I was bound to honour it. This was later to be the cause of a lot of conflict.

*   *   *

Every so often quite a few of the patients would go down to the visiting room to be interviewed by Dr Rolands and Mr Stewart. If all went well, a patient could be given his field or villa privileges, but it was common practice that a lad had to earn his field privileges before he was allowed to move from the block wards to a villa ward. When I had been in Rampton for 11 months, the usual crowd was sent down from E3 for the interview in the visiting room, and most of them came away with nothing. Then Mr Stewart issued another list of people to be interviewed — and my name was on it. I went down to the visiting room thinking I would be turned down for my villa privileges because the usual practice was that you were not considered for your villa until you had been in Rampton for at least two years. Happily I was proved wrong, and I found out afterwards that I was one of the first patients, if not *the* first, to receive his field and villa privileges within his first year. Three days later I was taken from E3 to Cedars Villa.

CEDARS VILLA

I soon found out that you had much more freedom to move around the villas as you pleased — but you still had to maintain a proper respect for authority. If you were ever heard calling staff anything but Sir, you were in trouble.

*   *   *

The Rampton villas are much bigger than a block ward. Each has a cloakroom leading into a big lounge; to the right of the lounge there is an office-cum-storeroom, a bedroom and a dayroom, and on the left a kitchen, another bedroom and a dining room. Just before you enter the lounge there is a stairway going up to a bathroom, drying room and staff toilet, then a few more stairs leading to two staff rooms and 18 side rooms running along both sides of a long corridor, plus a storeroom and an attic.

As on the block wards, every patient was given a job to be done after each meal; mine was cleaning the dayroom which meant I spent most of my time decking the floor. During the day the villa patients worked in one of the occupational shops. At that time there were two shoe shops, two tailoring shops, a basket shop, a metal shop, a carpentry shop, an upholstery shop and a pottery shop. They're an essential part of Rampton as they supply the patients with clothing and working materials, and they're popular with patients, partly because the staff are fair and human, and partly because they give you the chance to make friends. When you were working in the shop you could meet and talk to your friends without the occupational staff making crude suggestions, as some of the nurses were wont to do. All in all the shops gave you a reasonable degree of freedom, and relieved a lot of tension.

Between work and bedtime at 6.30, you could watch television in the lounge — although patients weren't allowed to switch it on until after 5.00 — or go into the dayroom to play darts or billiards or just listen to the radio. In the villa dormitories you had a bed, side-locker and a chamber pot, exactly as in the block ward.

Having been on E3 I knew a few of the other patients as most patients who were in Cedars Villa had come from E3. I also made a friend of Robert whom I knew to talk to in the occupational shops. All told, life was much easier on Cedars; there were usually only two staff on at any one time, and they were of the old school. Mr Cochrane for instance was very near retiring age, and although he had a reputation he seemed to be mellowing in his old age.

25

Depending on your record, once you moved from the blocks to the villa area you had the opportunity to earn a trusted job. In Rampton you had to earn everything you got, but it was worth it as a trusted job meant exactly that. It was not long before I was given a trusted job in the VR (which stood for visiting room and staff restaurant). That was where I met Gordon, an elderly nurse with a heart of gold; because I was able to work for such a good boss, life in Rampton became much more pleasant, although the visiting room side of the job was very upsetting for me at times as I had no family to come and see me.

There were some funny times too — there had to be or you would become completely unbalanced, and that would be the end of you. I remember walking into the dining room one day and seeing a small grey-haired charge nurse with a plate in one hand and a duster in the other. Polishing the plate with his duster he said: 'That's better, now you look like a nice clean plate. In fact you *are* a nice clean plate'. It was so unbelievable, I just stood there and laughed.

There were other things too, like the time I was told to light a fire with liquid paraffin which cleared the visiting room out in minutes, or a nurse pretending to look for eggs when he heard me laugh (I've got the kind of laugh which most people find funny — hence the joke about laying eggs). Silly but laughable things.

* * *

I'd never been to the weekly dance since arriving at Rampton, but once on Cedars I decided to give it a try. The dance was held on Thursday afternoons from 2.30 till 3.30 in the main hall which was also used as a picture hall and for church services. I had been in the hall when it was set out for church, but found that services were being used for the wrong purposes — for example it was a good excuse for lovers to meet. There was also the fact that patients who went to church regularly in the morning were made to feel that they were trying to get out of cleaning the ward and were penalised. I stopped going for these reasons, and found my comfort alone in my side room, or through talking to Dr Richardson.

Rampton being Rampton, even the weekly dance was kept under very tight control. Male patients would sit on one side of the hall and the female patients on the other side, with the staff posted at various points around the hall. When the records were put on, three staff would go out into the middle of the hall and stand in a line. The men would then go over to the women's side of the hall, but we weren't allowed beyond the rows of chairs on their side. Each couple would then start dancing, if you could call it that. We danced one foot apart, holding hands and all going round the hall in the same direction. We were not allowed to go in between the staff who were standing dead in line in the centre of the hall, and if a couple did, or got too close together, they were kicked off the floor and taken out. However, where there's a will there's a way, so the couples used to bunch up which gave everyone the opportunity for a quick kiss and feel and the passing of love letters.

Dances were the only time the sexes were able to mix — even the picture shows were on at separate times for men and women. Could you imagine being locked up in an all-male environment, seeing females once a week, being so near yet so far? More patients got into trouble over these dances than any other single thing, and I never went again.

Christmas was around the corner. I had just had my 21st birthday and there was no news of my family. My appearance and cleanliness were becoming sloppy, my interest in the stamp collection and work were falling off. I needed to have a laugh, yet all I seemed to be doing was weeping and living in a make-believe world.

Christmas should be a time of goodwill, happiness and brotherly love. The carols and songs of Christmas had so much warmth that they brought me some relief. Otherwise I felt that Christmas need not have come.

I needed a new interest, or I wasn't going to make it through the year, and by a fortunate coincidence I was asked if I'd like to join the Young Pioneers group on Cedars. Mr Stewart said this was OK, and it gave me the interest I needed to stop me going downhill. All the Young Pioneers were the right age to join the scouts — but the Scout Association wouldn't allow an official scouts group to be set up in Rampton. The name Young Pioneers was used to get over this problem, and we took part in all the activities an ordinary scouts group would get involved in — within the limitations of Rampton. We also had speakers including Ken Stokes, the referee. His talk was so interesting that I decided that I would like to become a referee myself. I liked playing football, but because I had two left feet, as it were, I was very rarely picked to play. Refereeing sounded ideal. I made a formal request about training to become a referee, and nearly received punishment on D1 for daring to ask such a thing.

A couple of weeks later, I was once again on the verge of being transferred to D1 for pissing out of the dayroom window. The nurse on duty was mad about cowboy films, and just before a western came on TV he would lock all the doors leading into the lounge. Any patient who was in the dayroom, lounge or toilets would just have to stay there until the film was over. Shortly after the film started on the day in question I wanted to leave the dayroom where I was working at my stamp collection to go to the toilet. I wasn't allowed to, and when I couldn't wait any longer I went out of the dayroom window. Just as I was doing this who should pass by but Mr Stewart. 'Bonehead, what do you think you're doing', he shouted. I was called into the office and asked for an explanation. After that the inner doors were never locked again, but I did receive two weeks punishment for what I'd done.

INTERNAL CONFLICT

By 1960/61 Rampton was beginning to show signs of unrest and there was bitter internal conflict between members of staff. The Mental Health Act 1959 was being implemented, which meant that patients could go in front of a new board called a Mental Health Review Tribunal and ask to be discharged. Many staff disagreed with this liberal reform as they had no way of knowing what was being said to the tribunal, and it was one of the very few rights patients had which staff had no control over. Until this time very few male patients had been released — it was always a big occasion when anyone went away — but the 1959 Act looked set to change all that.

★   ★   ★

The first sign that the honeymoon period was coming to a bitter end was that the younger staff were beginning to throw their weight about quite openly. The incident which made me realise this occurred early one evening when Chalky made a remark about a certain nurse's nickname, and Mr Matthews promptly kicked the hell out of him on the office corridor. When the grey-haired charge nurse came out of the office, Mr Matthews said he had been attacked. Chalky was bleeding quite badly, and I never did see how it finished because I had to go into the small reading room out of the way or I would have fainted, as I had so often done at the sight of blood.

★   ★   ★

Young staff from outside the old tight-knit Rampton circle were being employed, which wasn't going down at all well, and the general unrest meant that the patients were more likely to be set upon — I could see this very clearly as I went round the hospital. Part of my VR job was to sort out the papers concerning visits, and Gordon would take me round all the villas and blocks to issue them. This gave me the opportunity to get to know most of the patients by name, face and reputation, and I also got to know more about Rampton and what was going on.

On one occasion a staff nurse opened the door to D1 without kicking it first, as was the usual practice. I went in in front of the staff and Gordon — and got a boot in the balls before Gordon could forewarn the D1 staff. Everything was OK; the horrible senseless sickly feeling of wanting to flake out soon passed. After Gordon had made sure I was all right, the senior staff who had kicked me said 'When you come to D1 that's just a taste of what to expect'. I had seen two horrible acts of violence and had heard of many more; I had been punched now and again, but this for nothing, Christ.

28

Gordon let me lie down in the staff restaurant for the rest of the afternoon. I went back to the ward at 4.00 as usual, and the charge nurse called me into the office and told me: 'Keep your mouth shut, Harding, and you'll be all right. It'll not happen again'. He must have guessed what was going on in my mind: I knew that a welfare officer was coming to visit me within a week and I had gathered by this time that certain parties outside Rampton were interested in my well-being. Patients who had friends in the right places — particularly in the NHS or the Home Office — would have an easier ride at Rampton. For example patients who were caught trading tobacco — as I was — were usually certain to get D1. All I got was a beating and two weeks extra work on the ward, plus loss of privileges which meant that after finishing the extra work I had to go to bed with nothing to read or do.

*   *   *

The early bedtime at Rampton had always caused a lot of discontent amongst patients, and Dr Rolands was trying to introduce a later bedtime as part of his reforms. Staff were beginning to discuss the new shift system quite openly and it was not long before I found out that 1 October was to be the starting date for the long day. Patients would be getting up at 7.00 am and going to bed at 9.30 pm, except on the children's ward, E1 and D1. The big stumbling block was that the Ministry of Health and the high-ranking medical and administrative officials at Rampton wanted to keep a split shift system, whereas the staff wanted to work a day on/day off shift. Mr Stewart openly stated that the staff would get their long day shift 'over his dead body', and the patients were getting the thin end of the wedge as usual while the internal struggle for power was going on.

Staff eventually got their day on/day off shift, and patients were allowed to stay up until 9.00 pm, although bedtime was officially 9.30. This was the first mistake the Ministry and the Home Office were to make; instead of moving Rampton forward their action was to turn the hospital into an even more God-forsaken and loveless place in a few years to come.

*   *   *

A clearer sign that Rampton was moving backwards rather than forwards came one Christmas Day in the early 1960s. Until that time, 25 December had been the patients' own day — within reason. There was no work; you could laugh, you could shout without being told to shut up or being given extra work for making a noise, and you could even speak in the dining room.

On the day in question we were having breakfast (Christmas Day was the only time we had fried eggs and bacon together, so this was special too), when a staff nurse came into the dining room and told us all to shut up. I carried on talking, and got punched three times in the face.

Each Christmas Day all the officials did a complete round of the wards, wishing all the patients a happy day and hope for the New Year. I made sure that I stopped Dr Rolands and said that I didn't wish to spoil his Christmas but that I had a complaint. I told him that a nurse had hit me three times in the face, so he referred me to Dr Murray for a full report. Dr Murray and Mr Stewart both interviewed me. My chin hurt, but as there were no marks I couldn't prove my case and the episode went down in my case file as allegation not proven. Mr Stewart interviewed me again the following day and told me: 'Bonehead, if you have any more complaints, come to me first. Don't make a fool of yourself again and you'll be all right'. Thank God there were no repercussions. I discovered later that certain parties interested in my welfare had put out word that I was not to be touched. Who they were I never found out.

*   *   *

29

Mr Cochrane was retiring in a couple of weeks' time, and the uncertainty as to who was taking over was rather unsettling. Although he had his odd ways, I preferred the devil I knew to the one I didn't. Senior staff nurses were being promoted, the old school was falling away and, Christ, the reputations some people had were well-founded. Take Mr Edwards. A patient on one of the villas threw a plant pot at a nurse; Mr Edwards went over to him with a big bunch of keys, and spine-dropped him. Spine-dropping is a daily form of 'treatment' in Rampton. The staff stands behind the patient, grabs hold of his neck or collar, and then kicks his feet from under him — letting go of the neck or collar at the same time. The patient crashes to the ground, hitting the bottom of his spinal area, and can't move for a few seconds — or longer, depending on how well the spine-drop is carried out. In every case the patient gets a terrific shock to his nervous system, and at its worst this violent act can cripple a man for life.

As if the spine-dropping wasn't bad enough, Mr Edwards then kept hitting the patient on the head with the keys. There was blood everywhere. Two staff carried the patient off to D1 in a laundry basket, which is about three feet long by two feet wide and two feet deep, dropping him every so often on purpose. I never saw him again. Considering that a member of the nursing staff always did the autopsy when a patient passed away — whatever the cause of death — it is any wonder that very little of what I saw ever came to light?

SAM

Visiting days were Saturday and Sunday, and families and friends could also see patients by appointment on the first and third Monday of the month between 2.00 and 4.30. Part of my VR job was to take the tea and biscuits round on visiting day, and then collect the dirty cups and clean up. Gordon or one of the other nurses collected the money as patients were not allowed to handle cash. Visiting days were special — you could feel the glowing warmth of fellow patients' happiness when they heard the greetings of loved ones, be it mother, father, brother, sister or whoever. At the end of visiting time, the tears of happiness were lovely to see. Later in the evening though I felt as lonely as I had at St Peter's, except that here I had no secret dad and I dared not show how low I was. I felt I had to find someone to love — someone who would love me in return.

* * *

At about this time, after many years of trying to find my family with the help of Mr Stevenson and Mr Stewart, my first bit of information came to light. As I was working in the visiting room one morning Mr Stewart called me into his office, and sat me down at the desk. He then showed me my birth certificate. When I looked at it I found out that I had a second name, John, so from that day I have always referred to myself as Leonard John Harding, and I sign formal letters L J Harding. Mr Stewart also gave me an address where my mother lived in 1950.

I wrote her a letter, with much difficulty, that same evening. What could I say, and how? I ended up writing:

> *My dearest Mother,*
>
> *This letter will come as somewhat of a shock, but this is your loving son Leonard writing to you. After all the time I have spent looking for you, Mum, I'm so pleased to be able to write to you this my first of many, I hope, letters.*
>
> *I so much want to see you, Mum. Thank God I've found you. If you are unable to arrange a meeting, I will do so.*
>
> *God bless you always Mother,*
>
> *Your loving son,*
>
> *Len XXXX*

31

Days turned into weeks, weeks turned into a month, and still no reply. Mr Stevenson was not giving up hope at this point, and he did one hell of a lot of work for me behind the scenes.

★   ★   ★

I needed someone to feel for, to belong to. I had friends on the villa, but I needed someone like my mother to fulfil this need to belong. I was delivering the visiting papers on E3 one day when I came into contact with the first person I had begun to get interested in since arriving at Rampton. I knew nothing about him, I hadn't spoken to him, but I had heard a nurse call him Sam. I didn't find him a particularly good-looking person, yet I seemed to want to know more about him.

It was a time of change on Cedars. Thanks to Bert, Mr Williamson became charge nurse and two new staff nurses came onto the villa; all were strict, but fair, which made life that much easier. A lot of new patients were brought in from E3 and one of them was Sam. He soon became the unofficial leader, the person others looked up to, were used by, or were made outcasts by. Until then I hadn't been accepted within the villa circle, partly through my own doing. Now things were changing. Sam took a liking to me; previously we had only passed the time of day while I was on my paper round, but now we had the chance to get to know each other. He also collected stamps so we had quite a bit in common.

Sam became my first friend in the villa, and he let me take part in his tobacco lending system. We were only allowed a certain amount of tobacco at any one time, and he would lend out an ounce for an ounce and a half back. I would keep some in my locker for him. Sam was a wise young one, and there was very little he didn't teach me about how to use the system and make life better for yourself without getting caught. I started doing odd jobs for him, like washing and ironing, then came the more dangerous favour.

By this time my ward job was to keep the drying room and bathroom clean. I was working in the drying room one evening when Sam asked me to lay a couple of blankets and sheets on the floor and then to keep look-out. If anyone was heading towards the drying room I was to let him know, and to try and stop them. I call this a dangerous favour, since under the new shift system there were nearly always three nurses posted on the villa. They had little to do, and often just wandered about.

I let Sam know everything was ready, and when he and his boyfriend Colin went in I shut the door and started scrubbing the floor in the corridor. This scene was to be repeated many times.

Life at this time couldn't have got much worse. I loved Sam so much; I was so near, yet so far. He knew how I felt towards him, and although I spent my days working, eating, sleeping Sam, so to speak, all he wanted was to be with Colin. For the first time in my life I loved another person — the fact that the person happened to be male rather than female didn't matter — and knowing that he knew and accepted my feelings, even to a small degree, was giving me the fulfilment I had needed so long.

Sleeping in the same dormitory as Sam and Colin was to either make or break me, and I didn't have to wait long to find out which. My bed was next to Colin's and Sam slept at the other end of the dormitory, so Sam would swop beds with me and I would keep look-out while Sam and Colin were in the same bed making love. This used to upset me so much, yet I couldn't refuse anything Sam asked of me or told me to do. Everything I did without question. I loved him and I was not about to lose him because of my jealousy. The hardest part was trying to talk nicely to Colin.

Swopping beds was not just a convenience for Sam and Colin; others would do the same as homosexuality was as common as the day was long in Cedars. On one such swop night involving three lads, someone put black boot polish in the vaseline tin so the next morning three people came out of the dormitory with red faces and black backsides. Of course this put paid to any swopping of beds for quite a while as a light was left on all night, and it meant going back to my drying room whenever Sam wanted a private place to meet Colin.

★   ★   ★

The charge nurse on Cedars asked me if I would accept the staff club job if I were offered it. If I took it I would have to be moved from Cedars to Firs Villa, and I would be paid £1.27 plus, on paper at least. This job is given to the most trusted person in Rampton, and I knew the offer meant that the authorities were thinking of transferring or discharging me within the next two to three years. I should think most patients in Rampton would have jumped at a chance like this, but the thought of leaving Sam was overriding the advantages of the opportunity I was being offered. Although I hated Rampton, for the first time in my life I had found happiness and a sense of belonging, and although Sam and I had not had sex, we had a relationship I was not prepared to let go of. I loved Sam, so I refused the club job. Later that afternoon I told him what I had done. He told me to take it if it was offered again, and promised that if I did he would show how grateful he was for all the favours I had done for him and Colin.

Mr Stewart came on his daily round that teatime, and called me into the office. Once there he didn't waste words: 'Bonehead, you will take the staff club job or I'm sure we can find a spare bed for you in D2'. I was glad that Sam had told me to take the job as I was not too sure if this was just an idle threat. I told Mr Stewart that I was sorry I had refused this opportunity, and that I would accept the trust and faith he was placing in me. On the Sunday I was interviewed by Dr Rolands and was told that I would be transferred the next morning and would start work on the club job in the afternoon. Sam told me to clean my drying room out on Sunday afternoon, and that's when I knew all the heartache had been worth it. Sam fixed the door so that everyone would think it was locked, and we spent over an hour making love. Until then I had heard of a world trip, but didn't understand what it meant. I do now.

★   ★   ★

Firs Villa was a lot different from Cedars. Apart from four or five patients, most of the lads were in the 30 upwards age group, and there was a much more tense atmosphere than on Cedars. I had heard of Albert Perkins, the master of escape from Rampton, but this was the first time I had been on the same ward as him. We became very good friends. Jack, who I knew from E3, was also in Firs, and he and his mate had set up an illegal intercom from the ward office to his portable radio. Only a few of us knew about this bug, and we got to know every move in the hospital before it happened.

The club job meant I had a variety of things to do, including cleaning out the staff swimming pool, which made it very worthwhile and interesting. Instead of cleaning floors with deckers, like on the wards, I was able to use a proper cleaning machine.

While working at the club I came across quite a lot of club tickets and partly-filled glasses of beer and such like, but didn't touch anything until Mr Yeats, the charge nurse on Firs, told me to discreetly collect the tickets for him. By doing so, I was risking D1, but if I refused my life could be made hell anyway. In the same week Albert asked me to collect up the left-over beer, and I agreed.

★   ★   ★

On one of his rounds Mr Stewart called me into his office and told me that the letter I had written to my mother had been returned marked 'Not known at this address'. I felt I needed Sam more than ever, and at least seeing him twice a day as I went to and from work was a blessing. We were also able to pass each other love letters at these brief meetings.

That Christmas was the first I had looked forward to as Sam had written in one of his letters that we would be going to bed for 15 minutes when I went over to Cedars on Boxing Day. How this was arranged I don't know, but I have a good idea, and the thought of someone owning Sam like that was horrible. However, it meant we were going to be together and that's what mattered to me. Christmas came, and oh my God, if I could have given Sam the earth I would have. I worshipped the ground he walked on, and he had given me the fulfilment I had needed for so long. From now on I was Sam's, soul, body and mind, but we could never be together.

The week after Christmas I got so low, I think if it hadn't been for my fondness of Sam I would have asked God's forgiveness and called life a day.

*　　*　　*

While I was apart from Sam, the only thing that kept me going was my interest in my job. There was another lad working with me, and when he was off I had all his jobs to do. Rushing about one morning while I was cleaning out the swimming pool, I fell in fully clothed, which at first was frightening. When I got out I was wet through, but as I hadn't been in a swimming pool since I was a young lad, I decided to jump back in and have a swim. It was not until I had to get out to go over to the club that I began to worry about being the laughing stock of the hospital, and about what might happen to me for falling in. I could quite easily lose the job, and I didn't know whether to be upset or to treat the whole thing as a joke. Mr and Mrs Bailey, who were in charge of the staff club, decided for me and treated it as one big joke, so I never had any explaining to do. I was given some spare clothes to wear, and became the first patient in Rampton to wear private clothing for a complete day, which was rather funny. Two months later, however, I had another accident, and another reason to be grateful to Mr and Mrs Bailey.

Backing into the storeroom with the cleaning machine, I didn't notice that the trap door to the cellar was open, and before Mr Bailey could shout out, I fell through, letting go of the machine which fell across the hatchway. Mr Bailey was able to lean over and grab hold of my hand before I let go of the side. Mr and Mrs Bailey pulled me up, sat me in a chair and gave me a drink as I was white and shaking all over. I was taken by wheelchair to the hospital block for a check-up, just in case I had been hurt. The hospital block is the only part of Rampton where the name 'hospital' *means* 'hospital'.

Later that week I was interviewed by Dr Rolands about being transferred back to Powick. I refused. Much as I hated being in Rampton, no way was I going back to a hospital that had sent me to Rampton on bumped-up allegations — once bitten twice shy — and in any case I couldn't bear the thought of leaving the only person I'd ever loved. I told Sam what I'd done, and he didn't mind.

*　　*　　*

Around this time I received three pieces of news, and the first at least was good. Out of the blue I had a letter from a solicitor in Malvern informing me that I had been named as a benefactor in an old lady's will. I couldn't recall the lady, so I asked the charge nurse to investigate the matter for me. Some time later I was informed that I *was* the right person, and that the deceased lady was, in fact, one of the two elderly ladies I had worked for while I was still at St Peter's.

The next two pieces of news couldn't have been worse. After all Mr Stevenson's hard work, time, trouble and concern, and the efforts of others, my mother had been found. I was sent to E1 to see Mr Stevenson one Tuesday, and he had the sad duty to inform me that my blessed mother would not have anything to do with me: there would be no photograph, no letter, no visit, nothing. I was told that she'd married and had three more children, and it would do more harm than good if she were to let it be known that I existed. Good God, all I wanted to do was to see her once to fulfil the yearning to belong — surely that was not too much to ask.Reluctantly I agreed that if I was told what area she lived in I would not attempt to get in touch with her — not that I was given much to go on, but my word is my bond. Damn my word; if only I hadn't given it. Damn bloody Rampton.

Some weeks passed and Sam was transferred onto Firs Villas. What a nice change this made for me: I was so pleased to be with him again. He told me to write and accept the transfer to Powick, and promised that I could eventually live in the north near him. This made me so happy. Within a few weeks Sam got his discharge and left on a Saturday afternoon. How I cried.

Just before he left he gave me his address and phone number, and until my transfer to Powick three months later I broke one of Rampton's golden rules once a week. On Sunday mornings I would ring Sam from the telephone just outside the staff club. I handed in any money I found, but kept back sufficient for the weekly call which I looked forward to so much.

3. TROUBLED TIMES

OUT OF RAMPTON'S SHADOW

Leaving Rampton on 3 October 1965, I felt excited on the one hand yet frightened on the other. Travelling from Nottinghamshire to Worcestershire was such a terrifying experience that when I got back to Powick I was so nervous I couldn't speak properly. It was my first outing since early 1959, and everything seemed so big and fast and noisy.

My escort of two staff led me to the main entrance and we were met by a tall lean man who said he knew nothing about a Mr Harding coming from Rampton and asked us to sit in a small waiting room. Mr Harding, ha! Some time later the same man came back and introduced himself as the deputy chief male nurse. He welcomed me to Powick, saying he hoped I was pleased to be back, and assured me that I would be well looked after there. I was unable to speak without a bad stutter, and didn't answer.

I was taken to the male admission ward, M1. The ward had been altered and modernised, but the charge nurse who met me was the same man who had been on M1 before I went to Rampton. Each time he asked me a question I answered 'Sir this . . . Sir that'. He told me nowadays nobody said 'Sir' anymore and told me to relax. I was then taken into a small bedroom with a bed, wardrobe, side-locker, chair, carpet, mirror and armchair — so comfortable and homelike compared to Rampton. Not long after, a doctor came to examine me and told the charge nurse to give me some tablets as I was so nervous. Later that afternoon the charge nurse told me I could get up when I liked and sit in the ward, but I didn't go out of my room except for tea. I needed time to stop wanting to hear the shouting and the other familiar noises of Rampton. The change from one environment to another was incredible — the people were so warm, polite and friendly here, it was unbelievable. I was going to stick out like a sore thumb. Most of my manners, politeness and day-to-day common respect had gone. I began to panic: I'm not going to be able to adjust . . . People being so equal, its unreal . . . How could I not trust them? No I'd better not, these people sent me to Rampton in the first place . . . I'll phone Sam and let him know I'm out.

The third day at Powick I met Dr Grant, the doctor who put me in Rampton. One word from him and I could be sent back, so I tried to be nice to him instead of telling him how I really felt about the injustice of being sent to Rampton. Then I got the shock of my life. He told me that a mistake had been made. If I kept my nose clean for a month he would have me taken off all compulsory orders, and then I could find a job and lodgings and have my discharge.

★   ★   ★

While on M1 I was given an opportunity to work in the occupational centre, which I enjoyed as just sitting about doing nothing all day is not me. After three weeks I progressed to M3, a ward for men who were to be trained to go back into the outside world, and was put on domestic duties which meant I received a lot more money. I had a new doctor too — Dr Wyatt, whom I recall seeing in Rampton.

I hadn't been on M3 long when I awoke one night to find the dormitory filling with smoke. I opened the door into the main ward and it was worse, so I set off the fire alarm, opened the fire door and started to shout for everyone to get out quickly. Within seconds staff were in the ward moving us all out. I found out later that the fire was started by a patient accidentally leaving a burning cigarette in his pocket.

On my first day out from Powick I visited Mr Mullock's grave and St Peter's Church. A flood of memories came floating back, Powick and Rampton disappeared like a bad dream, and peace of mind and contentment set in. I decided to go to St Peter's Home in the late afternoon, but when I got to the gate I couldn't go in. I walked up and down Cowley Road, just outside the home, then took the route I used to take from the home to work in 1958. I felt so drained when I got back to Powick I had to go to bed. I never went out again until just before Christmas.

* * *

Ringing Sam twice a week and receiving his letters was heaven, but I needed to see him, so when he invited me up to Grimsby for the New Year, I didn't need to be asked twice. I quickly wrote out my 72 hours notice — by now this was all I needed to do if I wanted to spend some time away from the hospital as I was a voluntary patient. Dr Grant had kept his word.

I bought a new suit and other clothing just before Christmas, and packed everything I needed a week in advance. I spent a very enjoyable Christmas at Powick, which surpised me as Christmas is usually such a low time for me, and on New Year's Eve I travelled from Worcestershire to Grimsby. The only part of the journey I hated was the stop at Retford — it was too near the hole for my liking. I arrived at Grimsby at 6.35 pm and there was Sam waiting for me in his van. We drove to his place and stopped for over an hour — an hour of sheer delight, and then went looking for lodgings. After some time we stopped off at the main Grimsby police station as Sam said they would have a list of places there. Within an hour I had found lodgings, then Sam and I went out for a while as it was New Year's Eve.

Saturday and Sunday were long lonely days as I didn't see Sam, and on Monday things were even worse. I was in a world I knew nothing about, and being lonely I rang Bert, but he was too busy at work to talk to me. I got lower and lower, and I knew I just couldn't make it on my own. I rang the local welfare office but I was not on their books so they could do nothing for me. Sam was too busy to see me. The welfare office didn't want to know. Who could I turn to? Then I saw a police station.

I asked the sergeant at the desk if he could put me in touch with anyone as I needed help. I was taken into a room and given a cup of tea, and the sergeant came in and sat with me. Next came a mental welfare officer who took me to his office in Grimsby. He told me that as I was not on their books he had rung Powick; I was to make my own way back there, or I would be taken back to Rampton. I rang Sam. He told me I could stop with him for the night and promised to see I caught the first train in the morning. Three days outside and I had failed. I went back to Powick.

When I arrived at Powick they were not expecting me and were not going to accept me back. Christ, I was not going to Rampton again. The charge nurse on M1 admitted me on a voluntary basis until a ruling had been made. Dr Wyatt put me on her books, but it was nearly a month before I dared go out of Powick without an escort. I kept in touch with Sam though. He told me that my premium bonds and other things I had left with him were safe and that when I was ready to return to Grimsby, I would be welcomed.

*   *   *

I was soon back on M3, and I hadn't been there long when I had my first test as to how I would react in a tight corner. One evening two patients came into my room and started pushing me about and breaking my records. I was determined to stand up for myself, although I knew that if anything happened I would be the guilty party. I spine-dropped the bigger of the two, and got no more trouble — in fact all three of us became good friends after this episode. Unknown to us, one of the night nurses was in the corridor outside listening to what was going on, but nothing was ever said.

It was good to have friends at Powick, and it gave me much more confidence. Each weekend I would go into town with Bill or Geoff or another friend, Pam. I was now getting used to the outside world, although the only time I went out on my own was to visit the Master's grave. As I didn't have a job I did a lot of walking in the hospital grounds, and on one of my evening walks I ended up by the pool. I saw a female patient in the middle swimming — or so I thought until I got closer. The water wasn't very deep — it only came up to my waist — so I waded in and grabbed hold of her. By the time I got near the side of the pool two female nurses had arrived, and they took her back to her ward. Some years later she died in Rampton.

In March I got a job outside the hospital cleaning cars from 8.00 am till 5.00 pm Monday to Friday, but the long days on my own in the carwash affected me so badly that after three weeks I had to be taken back to Powick and lost my job. Within the confines of Powick I felt secure, yet I needed to belong to the real world. I knew I had to find answers to my problems if I was ever to lead a normal life. Some of these problems I had created myself, but Powick and Rampton had done little to help. Rampton had turned me into a mixed-up, institutionalised, frightened human being who trusted no-one but Sam, even though I knew deep down that this shouldn't be so. I'd been out of Rampton for six months, yet I still couldn't shake off this fear and twisted bitterness.

I had to find another job and wondered whether I could get into the forces. I had no criminal record, I was young, fit and tidy, and my word was my bond; it could be the making of me, sort me out. First I had to get out of Powick and find a job, then I could apply for a post in the forces. Looking through the local paper about a week later, I came across a vacancy for a night porter in a local hotel, so with the consent of Dr Wyatt and some help from a welfare officer I applied. I got the job, but only after quite a long and misleading interview. I told my boss-to-be that I was in Powick because I had had a nervous breakdown, and that I could produce a doctor's letter stating that I was fit again. I had told a white lie, but I knew that if I told the full truth I would be turned down as I had been before.

The job entailed starting at 5.00 pm, helping out in the kitchen, washing up, attending to new guests and so on. From 7.00 till 11.30 pm I did room service and from 12 midnight to 6.00 am I polished shoes, cleaned the toilets, went on security rounds and collected the morning papers. From 12.30 onwards I was the only person on duty, and from 2.00 am till 4.00 am I was supposed to have a break. However I overslept one time, so I altered my shifts to suit my convenience: I would do a couple of hours at a time then take a ten minute break, which worked out much better

40

all round. The pay was quite good: I received full board plus £9.00 in wages each week, and some weeks I made more in tips than pay. I loved this night job, and it's a pity I couldn't have allowed myself to break with my past and hold on to it.

Most nights I had a couple of the local bobbies round for a cuppa, and I was glad of the company. I must say the police were always very kind and helpful. I only had to call them if I thought I heard an intruder and they would come immediately. They were very efficient. One night I asked the sergeant if there was any possibility of me joining the police force as this had been my ambition for a long time. I told him all about my past, which he promised not to reveal to my boss, and he said I couldn't join the police force as I had been in Rampton, even though I had no criminal record. However, he thought I could get into the armed forces.

After three weeks as a night porter, I hadn't been any further than Powick to visit Pam. I decided to venture out and get to know Worcester a bit better, and it was on one of these walks that I came across the armed forces careers office. I walked in and within three hours I was told to give the hotel my notice; I'd been accepted for the army, subject to a medical. I went for the medical the next week, and I told the truth about my past. I passed a medical, physical and educational test, and the day I signed on for nine years in the Grenadier Guards was the proudest moment in my life. Colour Sergeant Petty, who had taken me for the test and escorted me for my medical, said 'Welcome to the Guards' and those words filled me with pride. At last I felt I was a part of a system I would be able and willing to fit into. However, when I reported to the careers office to collect my travel warrant to Purbright, Surrey, the next day, I was informed by a major that I couldn't be accepted, although I had signed on for nine years, and that no other regiment would have me. I was dumbfounded. Why, what's wrong with me? I'm back where I was in 1958 — a nobody with nothing. It's unfair.

Sergeant Petty got my job back for me, but my heart wasn't in it any longer. I couldn't face going back to tell them at Powick — I would have been the laughing stock. I rang my only friend, Sam, who told me that in a month there would be plenty of jobs up in Grimsby and that I could stop with him in his room until I found lodgings.

*　　*　　*

Two weeks later I was about to start my shift at the hotel when the boss informed me that a Detective Sergeant Waterson had called in to see me while I was off duty. From what the boss told me I realised that Sergeant Waterson had wanted to talk to me about Sam. I phoned Sam but his mother answered and told me that Sam had been taken into police custody charged with stealing a watch. I immediately went to the local police station and gave Sam an alibi by saying that I had sent him the watch for his birthday. Back at work I rang Sam's mother again and was told that Sam was being taken to court in two days' time. Next morning I asked my boss for my cards and wages. I got my wages, but not my cards, and went to the local police station to let them know I was leaving, as I had been told to do. I packed and left for Grimsby.

I arrived in Grimsby at 4.30 pm and was met by Sam's brother, who told me the whole story. A lot more was involved than I knew about. However, I had committed myself, and when Sam was allowed out on bail until the case came to court, I lost all second thoughts about getting involved.

Meeting Sam again seemed so odd. It had been five months since I had last seen him and he had changed, although in bed he was more exciting than ever. His behaviour and appearance had altered so much that the difference between us affected me badly when I was not in his company, yet when we were together, no matter what he said or did, I lost all self-control and couldn't question anything he asked of me. I just seemed to worship the ground he walked on.

The first week in Grimsby I spent every day looking for a job so I didn't see as much of Sam as I would have liked. While looking for work on the seafront (if you can call the River Humber estuary a seaside!) I met Albert Perkins, whom I had known in Rampton. He offered me lodgings and a job where he was working, but I refused his kind offer — a decision I was soon to regret. We had a long talk and a drink and he warned me to stay away from Sam. How I was to regret not taking this warning, or the many others I had had.

A WICKED AND APPALLING CRIME

Nearly a week after I arrived in Grimsby the Labour Exchange sent me along to a bakery where I got a job as a machine operator, even though I had never seen one of these machines before in my life! I was living with Sam's family, and his mother would make me sandwiches to take to work and cook a meal for me at night. I enjoyed the job and the split shift system, and was receiving a good wage packet. On pay day I would take so much out for my rent and £5.00 for my pocket money. The rest Sam had. One may think that I was buying Sam's friendship, but in fact giving him money saved him from stealing.

None of Sam's family knew about our relationship or our financial arrangements and his criminal acts. Once a week, at least, I was given instructions for an alibi in case he needed one. In order to keep my word to him I had to all intents and purposes become a liar. I was leading two lives, yet no life at all. I began losing weight and my work output suffered. I started to smoke like a chimney, and for what? Things came to a head when I saw something I shouldn't have. Oh God, I didn't want to believe what I had seen. That night I decided to move out of Sam's place, and three days later found lodgings with Dave and Brenda and their three young kids. In general things seemed to get better: the short time I was to lodge with Brenda gave me a wonderful insight into what family life was all about, and I enjoyed babysitting with the kids. I made other friends, in particular a young man I met on the beach. This time I felt everything was right, and for a while I seemed contented to be with him, yet I still allowed myself to be at Sam's beck and call. The conflict within me made me my own worst enemy, and in a moment of reality I cried out for help. I rang one of the staff at Rampton, but before I was put through, I replaced the receiver.

★   ★   ★

I had been in Grimsby for about three months when I took part in a wicked and appalling crime. At this stage of the book I had intended to go into great detail about this terrible crime. However, on consideration I feel that to do so would be totally unreasonable, and could only bring further grief to the family and friends of the elderly lady who was murdered. Therefore I am just going to touch on the shocking event and, by doing so, you may think I am trying to belittle what took place. No way could I do this: my shame and guilt are too great.

★   ★   ★

While I was still in a terrible state over my relationship with Sam, I met up with Tom, another ex-patient from Rampton. I was grateful for his affection, and when he asked me to take part in robbing an elderly lady, I agreed. I knew the lady and she had been kindness itself to me, and I hoped that if I was there the lady wouldn't be harmed. This was not to be.

After this senseless crime took place, I decided rightly or wrongly that I would go to the police and take full blame — I had given Tom my word that I would never let anyone know he was involved too. I had heard on the radio and read in the local paper that the police were looking for two people, but the descriptions didn't fit either of us. I knew I had to go to the police as more and more people were being directly and indirectly hurt by what we had done. It was too late, I know, but I realised I was not fit to be in society.

The talk in the changing room when I got to work was of the murder. I went to see the works manager and told him that I had been at the old lady's place on the afternoon of the crime, and asked him what I should do. He called the police and two policemen from the local CID came to see me in his office. After talking to them for a while, I made a statement to the effect that I was at the scene of the crime, also dropping hints that I hoped would make them feel I needed looking at more closely. I carried on working the shift out, but I didn't get much done. I then went back to my lodgings and dozed for an hour, but I couldn't sleep so I went for a walk. I hadn't gone far when the two policemen I had seen at the bakery stepped out from a little alleyway and asked me if I would care to go with them.

I went with the police to a van and they took me back to my lodgings where I met Mr Miller-Patrick and Mr Carmichael, who were in charge of the case. Mr Miller-Patrick asked me if he and Mr Carmichael could enter my room; I agreed. On the way up Mr Miller-Patrick 'accidentally' bumped into me and gave me a quick frisk to make sure I wasn't carrying any weapons. I thought to myself, he knows his job. After a light search of my room and a few simple questions about the statement I had made, they asked me if I would allow them to take some of my clothing away, and if I would mind going with them to Grimsby police headquarters.

*　　*　　*

At my first interview I was told that I needn't say anything or make any statements unless I wanted to, and that I could, at any time, ask for a solicitor to be present. After this interview I was put in a room with a Detective Inspector Blakeman, an elderly policeman I took an instant liking to. We didn't discuss what I was there for, but talked instead about his career, my background, and life in general. It turned out that he had arrested 'Crafty' Cunningham in Grimsby in 1954. I remembered the Cunningham case well, because he was supposed to have knocked two women off their bicycles in the Malvern area. The local policeman had come up to St Peter's in the course of his enquiries, and that was one of the things that gave me the idea of wanting to be a policeman. During our discussion I asked Blakeman about Miller-Patrick. Off the record we had a long and deep talk, and I decided that I was going to come clean as I felt I could trust his authority. However, by the time Mr Miller-Patrick had been called back, I had had time to think about my word being my bond and the backlash if I told the truth.

I was then formally told of my rights, and I made up a story around the truth. Later that day I overheard one policeman make a remark about me being a 'bloody nutter', and then I realised they knew I was lying to them.

*　　*　　*

During my first two days in custody, I made five statements and gave them sufficient evidence to convict me. When I was charged, I was asked if I would like a solicitor to be present. I declined, although I knew I would have to have one to accompany me into court. Mr Carmichael and Mr Miller-Patrick assured me that they would see I got legal representation. They were as good as their word, and got me a lady solicitor who had a very good reputation.

On the Saturday night I was put in an open cell. There relief came, and I fell into a deep sleep until very late on the Sunday. The next thing I knew, there were six policemen in my cell and one was talking about what a doctor had been saying. From then until the Tuesday, there was a two man team to look after me — I was never left on my own or locked in the cell. The policemen just didn't sit by the door; they played cards and were really very good to me. One sergeant in particular was more like a father than a policeman. I couldn't have been treated any better if I had been on the right side of the law, and this fact was to be of great help to me in the future.

The day I went to court, I was supposed to have been in court helping Sam with the case about the watch. I was remanded in police custody, and taken to Lincoln Prison later that afternoon. At Lincoln I was taken into the reception area at the same time as another prisoner was brought in, and we were both put into wire-netting cells. The police went into the reception office with the prison officers, and then two prisoners with red bands on their arms came and asked me who I was. I said my name and was told to stand over by the wall, and then they asked the other prisoner what his name was. He was taken in for a bath, and one could hear the noise. When I went in for my bath, I was told that if I kept my ears and eyes shut I would be all right. I fully expected to get fixed, but I wasn't touched. I then changed into prison uniform, my own clothes were taken away, and I was escorted to the hospital block.

I had never been in prison before and was amazed at the wire-netting between each landing (as I found out they were called). I kept calling everyone Sir, as I had always been used to doing, and this showed a lot of the others how green I was. However, I called these officers Sir as a mark of respect for them and their uniform, not out of fear and intimidation as in Rampton.

* * *

The committal date was set: it had taken a very long time. The police were as good to me as they had always been. However, I was to repay their kindness very shabbily. After the committal procedure, I was taken back to Grimsby police headquarters. There I was given a meal, but when it was time for me to go back to Lincoln Prison I dropped the books the police had kindly given me and started to run through the back door. I was brought down by a flying rugby tackle, and taken back to the charge room. I was asked why I had done it, but why I ran, where I was going, and what for, I don't know. I can only put it down to shame and fear. Shame for the part I had played in this appalling crime, and fear that they would find out I was lying, because I had given my word. The strongest remark the police made to me was that I was a fool.

I went back to Lincoln Prison, and until the trial I was classed as an escapee and put into 'patches'. (This means wearing a prison uniform with bright yellow patches on the jacket and trousers: the patches can't be removed and this is a good form of security because you'd really stick out if you were to escape.) I had my fingerprints and photograph taken, I was moved to a different cell every three days, and wasn't allowed out of the cell without an escort and without an officer signing for me wherever I went. The hospital block staff were very good and allowed me to move fairly freely to and from the games room which was situated over the hospital block, but a shortage of officers meant I couldn't go to evening classes, pictures or church. My daily exercise was also quite restricted, but I know for a fact that some officers made an extra effort to see I had at least half an hour's exercise per day.

Whilst in Lincoln Prison, I was interviewed by Dr Abbott, the prison doctor and a doctor from another area, who had to make medical reports on me for the prosecution and defence solicitors. It was obvious that neither believed my statements. I then got a very unpleasant shock when a doctor from Rampton came to interview me. He made it quite clear that he didn't believe me either. He did believe I had had a part to play in this terrible crime, but he obviously thought that what I said I had done was not consistent with my normal pattern of behaviour. I was asked to explain how the same person could stop a woman drowning herself, wake up a ward full of patients and get them to safety from a fire, and then ruthlessly kill an elderly lady, all within the space of five months. It didn't make sense. I had no answer except to say that I had made my bed and had to lie in it.

His visit was my first indication that I was going to be sent back to Rampton. The more I thought about it, the less I liked it, but looking back at everything that had happened, it was no more than I deserved.

* * *

On 31 October 1967 I went up to Lincoln Assizes. I was allowed to wear my own clothing and had to take my belongings with me as it was by now common knowledge that I would be sent to either Rampton or Broadmoor after pleading guilty to manslaughter on the grounds of diminished responsibility. I decided to plead this way because I thought it would give me a better chance of being sent to Broadmoor rather than Rampton.

I was called into the dock. I had seen a Crown Court in films and on television, but this was the first time I had been in one and it was frightening. I had two policemen with me, one in the dock and one by the top of the stairs. I was told to stand, my name and the charge were read out and I was asked 'How do you plead to this charge?'. I looked around to see if Tom was in court, as he had promised to be, but he wasn't. My solicitor made a remark to me, but I didn't hear it properly. I thought I was going to collapse. I heard someone say 'Read from the piece of paper', then I heard myself saying 'I plead not guilty to murder, but guilty to manslaughter on the grounds of diminished responsibility'. Everything was so to the point. The judge asked counsel whether they would accept this plea, and my counsel said something. Dr Abbott then read out his remarks, and those of the other doctor who had seen me, and I heard him say as clear as a bell that there was a bed ready for me in Rampton and an escort waiting to take me there. The prosecuting counsel then stated that the offence was entirely consistent with my background and that he wouldn't be calling for any statement from the police unless the judge thought it necessary.

While the judge was making his remarks, it occurred to me that I was not the only one using the three unheard allegations from 1959 to make sure I was convicted. I then said something which got mistaken for a statement 'Yes, mentally ill, Sir'. I was about to crack up, so I didn't say anymore. All I could see was Rampton D1 looming up.

* * *

I don't remember going back down to the cells. The next thing I knew I was sitting opposite Dr Abbott in a small interview room and he was asking if there was anything I would like to tell him. We both knew what he wanted to hear, and this time it would have been all so easy to tell him the whole truth, but oh God, I had given my word and therefore I had to take what I knew was to come, without self-pity. I couldn't undo what I'd done, and by now I was so confused that I

46

doubted whether I could have given Dr Abbott a clear picture of what had taken place if I'd wanted to. I was given two green tablets, and taken back to the cells.

About lunchtime I was told it was time to leave. The handcuffs were put on and I walked between two lines of policemen until I got to a car. There I was handcuffed to two prison officers, and with a police escort back and front, I was taken to Rampton.

4. RAMPTON 1966-77

*'While I'm in any form of authority you'll get nothing
because you're worth nothing'*

'WELCOME BACK TO THE FOLD, HARDING'

The officers in the car made the hour's drive much more bearable by keeping me talking and letting me smoke, but when I saw Rampton looming up I felt sick. I just closed my eyes and hoped my worst fears wouldn't come true. As we went into the main lodge, Mr Stewart came through and told the prison officers to get the handcuffs off as this was a hospital and there was no need for them. He didn't say anything to me.

Then my escort appeared, the officers handed me over, and the longest, hardest walk of my life began. As yet I hadn't been touched. The tablets Dr Abbott had given me must have taken effect as I felt numb from head to foot. We went into D1, where I'd thought I was going to be admitted, but when we got there I was knocked from one wall to another with the staff lined up, each having a punch or kick. I made it to the door of E1, a staff nurse opened it, and the kicking stopped. I was told to go through the door and not to move more than three steps, and then stand to attention. I stood there waiting for the worst to happen, but it didn't. I just got pushed between my escorts along E1 sick corridor and along the office corridor to the bathroom. Then it began. I could feel the punches and kicks, but was so numb I felt no pain. My private clothing was stripped off me, I was put in a cold bath and the wet towel treatment was used. This is the most terrifying form of 'treatment' at Rampton. A soaking wet towel is wound round the patient's neck and tied into a knot behind one ear. After some frightening moments, you pass out, and if the towel is kept there too long it can kill you. I blacked out at least three times, but by now I was past caring and the pain was starting to outdo the effects of the tablets I'd been given. How I got to the clinic room I don't know.

Sometime that afternoon a doctor gave me a medical, as was the procedure with all new patients. The staff nurse who escorted me to the treatment room told the doctor: 'This is the bastard who killed the old lady, but his mate isn't in here yet'. The doctor had a long stick, pointed at one end and round at the other, with which he made my feet bleed. I thought: 'If a doctor's at it, I will really go through it'.

I was then taken to the clinic and told to lift up my nightshirt. They dipped cotton wool into some white stuff and asked me where my mate was, and why he wasn't there. Each time I went to speak the white stuff was put on my private parts, which made them feel as if they were being burned. At

50

this moment I just wished I could die, but that would have been the easy way out. For hours after this my body ached and I was in pain all over.

Then came a flow of unofficial interviews. Mr Foster, a senior nurse, came in and didn't mince his words. 'While I'm in any form of authority Harding I'll see that you get nothing because you're worth nothing.' This remark was made good time and time again. I received visits from staff I didn't even know existed. Each person would strip my bed and give me some kicks or fist treatment, or both, and ask me where my mate was. The only people who did nothing more than make a remark were Mr Stewart who said: 'Welcome back to the fold, Harding', a charge nurse who called me a bastard, and another charge nurse who told me: 'Stop crying, it won't help you here'. I'm sure this remark was made out of kindness because I had learned from being in Rampton before that to show weakness only got you more hammer. My meals varied according to who was serving them. Sometimes there was so much salt on the food it was inedible.

On the second day I was taken to the tailors to be fitted out for clothing. I got the same sort of remarks about my mate and some fist treatment. On the third day I had my first official interview with Dr Saunders who was to be my responsible medical officer. I didn't know him by sight but I was aware of his name and reputation as Tom had been under him in Rampton. He came straight to the point: 'Your first 15 years you will do in D2 (Dolphin Ward). Why have you told all these lies? I don't believe a word of your statement. If you tell me the truth now I'll see what can be done. What part did you have in it?'. I thought I had made enough statements and given sufficient evidence to prove that I and I alone had committed the terrible crime. I realised during this interview that I had lied so badly no-one believed what I said. The irony of it was that I had lied to keep my word as my bond. I was pleased when the interview was over.

I spent the third day in bed. It was my worst day as the only person who spoke to me was another patient, and what he said was not very complimentary.

*　　*　　*

As a returnee I was expected to know the routine and I knew that if I did anything wrong I would be jumped on, and hard. On my first day up I got out of bed at about 10.30 am, and was taken to have a bath and then issued with a full set of hospital clothing, plus toothbrush, comb, hand-towel and locker key. I was told that if I lost anything I knew what to expect. The staff nurse and student in charge of the clinic corridor had me working up by D1 door decking the same piece of floor for the rest of the day. Only at dinner and teatime did I stop, and of course each time staff came down the corridor to or from D1 they gave me a bit of treatment — as it was called.

How pleased I was when dinner time came, although no-one really wanted to know me, which was quite understandable. Normally if there is anything about a Rampton patient in the papers or on television, the other patients are not allowed to see it, the reason being that no patient is supposed to know what another is in for. Judging by people's attitude to me, it seemed that this rule had either been altered or forgotten. Each time a patient is released from one of the special hospitals and then re-admitted because he has been involved in a crime, it hits the headlines. The Home Office and the DHSS then stop or put back any transfers or discharges in the pipeline for patients who've committed violent crimes like rape or murder, until public opinion is calm again. The infamous Graham Young case is the best example of this. I believe that it's only patients in special hospitals who suffer because of adverse publicity — prisoners are not affected in the same way.

I hope this explains why most of my fellow patients were less than pleased to see me — in fact it was people I knew from before who were the worst in their attitude. Thank God not everyone was so hard on me. Harry, a Londoner, knew what I was in for but adopted the attitude that no matter what I'd done, I was still a human being and he was not going to pass judgment as it wasn't his place to do so. I was very thankful that someone at this time was prepared to show me such kindness.

*　*　*

Until the crime I had loved going to church, but much as I wanted to go now, I couldn't allow myself the comfort I knew it would bring. The Rev Hewitt, who was the chaplain at Rampton, always visited all new inmates, and I was so grateful when he came to see me as I couldn't bring myself to ask to see him. Rev Hewitt has a very down-to-earth approach, and he was able to converse with me on a man-to-man level. We had a very long and frank discussion, and I got a lot of relief from this meeting.

The next day Mrs Martin, the welfare officer, came to see me. A thousand patients and one welfare officer, not a bad average! She asked if I wanted to put in an appeal, but I told her that as far as I was concerned there was no point. She then asked what I wanted done with the clothing the Grimsby police had taken from my room. I wanted the only evidence that counted destroyed, so I told Mrs Martin that all the clothing was to be burned. My bike was to be given to my landlady Brenda who had been so good to me.

*　*　*

I had only been away from Rampton for just over a year, but in my first few days back on the ward what I'd half suspected while I'd been in bed was confirmed. Rampton was altering, and fast. The charge nurse's word was no longer law; staff nurses and students seemed to have more say and to do what they wanted. There was no chain of command. Most of the old charges had gone, and those who were left were just finishing their time and showed no signs of disagreeing with the new trend at Rampton. Bert Stewart, once the little tin god of Rampton, had very little say in the day-to-day running of the place, although he still did his daily round. Rampton was falling apart, and I could see big trouble looming ahead. I just hoped it would crack the walls, so that the outside world could see Rampton for what it really was.

Needless to say, the patients were coming off worst in all this. Fists and boots were being used quite openly, without any just cause, and I wasn't the only patient who was having a rough ride. In fact Barry and Rob were having an even rockier ride than I. Unknown to a lot of staff and patients, the police had been called in because it was suspected that a gun was to be smuggled into E1 by the contractors building a new occupational complex inbetween E Block and D Block. The detectives were taking it in turns to watch from the top corridor leading between D and E Blocks. They must have heard or seen or at least suspected how the patients were treated, and yet they did nothing about it, as far as I know.

Nothing was ever found. However a gun *did* come into E1, but it was taken out again as the three patients who were going to use it to escape got split up. Obviously the staff must have realised what was going to happen. They knew Barry was involved, but couldn't prove it.

As for Rob, his face didn't fit from the moment he walked into Rampton, and the fact that he was mentally ill didn't help. Rampton had always been for patients who were psychopathic or mentally handicapped — and the staff just weren't able to deal with someone suffering from a mental illness. If they take a dislike to you in Rampton, you are a marked man and can do nothing right. I wasn't sure whether I was marked or whether I was still getting the backlash for being readmitted. Only time would tell.

*　*　*

Just before my first month was up, I was interviewed by Dr Rolands who was still medical superintendent. He didn't condemn me out of hand as many others had. I was asked again about my case, and he said he was sorry to see me back. I then received an internal letter stating that I was on a section of the Mental Health Act which meant I could only be released with Home Office permission. I could be detained for a year, or for the rest of my life.

* * *

Christmas came, and I received a card which simply said 'I'm with John, love Tom'. I also found out that someone came to visit me, but was not allowed to see me on Dr Saunders' orders. From what I had seen so far, there was no way I was ever going to get a fair deal out of Dr Saunders. We had differed on every subject we had gone into, and there was never going to be any compromise on either side. Knowing I couldn't meet him halfway, I decided in my own interest to get a change of responsible medical officer (RMO). I wrote to the Ministry of Health complaining that my visit had been stopped, using this to further my case for a change of RMO. I received a letter back stating that my visitor had been told she was not allowed to see me on medical grounds.

* * *

Dr Saunders came to E1 to interview me and told me that I was being transferred to D3, which is a combined ward (an official term) for patients who are mentally handicapped or epileptic. Mr Thompson was in charge on D3, the same Mr Thompson who had been second in charge on Cedars last time I was there. He said that there wasn't any need to read my notes as he knew me. Again, the people who should have felt let down by me were showing the least bitterness towards me.

WARD D3

The next day on D3, Mr Groves, Mr Vincent and Mr Samuels came on duty. I knew Mr Groves by reputation and sight only. They treated me in a cold, rough, indifferent way; I knew within the week that I was going to go through it, and I did.

I was put on cleaning toilets, as it's the usual practice at Rampton that new patients get the worst jobs on the ward. Each morning I was told to clean the back stairs, and Mr Vincent and Mr Samuels would then take it in turns to make black marks on the floor I had already scrubbed. 'You bastard, you missed this. Do it properly.' As I went to clean the black marks off, I would get some boot treatment. So much noise would be made that a staff nurse from D2 would come up to find out what was going on. As soon as he saw what was happening, he would say: 'If that bastard's playing up, give him some treatment and tell him not to make so much noise'. Then he would go, leaving me to receive more boot. Every time that shift was on, which was every other day, I would go through the same routine.

In the dormitory I was put to sleep next to the night room and light. Most nights a different staff nurse would be on, and I would be subjected to the same treatment. 'You bastard, where's your mate.' 'Get under your bedclothes.' Then I would get some boot or fist or both.

As on E1, I wasn't the only patient on the receiving end of this kind of treatment. I can't recall one day going by without at least two or three patients being made to suffer. As most of the patients on D3 were severely mentally handicapped or epileptic, one would expect quite a lot of violence which would be caused through their mental condition rather than any criminal leanings. There were always one or two patients in deep litter (this is when a patient is put in a side room wearing a canvas suit with the sleeves tied behind his back and given a shot of paraldehyde). Both staff and other patients would be attacked when one of the violent cases was in a bad mood, and this led to a violent environment, but I have to say in all fairness that there was a lot of unnecessary brutality. Staff obviously need to restrain a patient when he cracks up, but a line must be drawn between restraint and plain violence.

Until that point, I'd never seen a patient treated worse than SC, the policeman killer. Every day he would be kicked from one end of the corridor to the other, spine-dropped, his face rubbed in his own shit amongst many unhuman acts. God, he would have been better off dead — I know I would have wanted to be. As if this wasn't enough, the patient's doctor openly approved of this kind of treatment by putting words into SC's mouth about how all his injuries had been caused by accidents such as slipping on mats, falling out of bed and walking into doors. It was sickening. While SC had committed a terrible crime, probably worse than mine, no-one can justify this sort of treatment.

Then came an act of inhumanity that put me in mind of the Gestapo during the Second World War. Tony was an unlikeable person, through no fault of his own. His looks didn't help him, he was an epileptic and he was incapable of hiding his homosexuality. He was therefore disliked from the moment he walked into Rampton from a local hospital. He had no criminal record; he had been wrongly accused of ripping the snooker table cloth. On the occasion in question, the stand-in charge nurse, Mr Hillman, told Tony to stand outside the office door and called some of the other patients up from the dayroom. 'Throw this bastard up to the ceiling until I tell you to stop, and the first one to walk away will get the same.' Six of us — yes I was one — picked him up from the floor after Hillman had spine-dropped him, threw him up in the air and let him drop. Three times this happened. Then he was kicked into a side room by Mr Hillman and two other staff and left there until the next day when the ward charge nurse sent for the doctor. Tony was taken to an outside hospital with a broken arm, plus other bruising, and it was nearly two months before he was back on D3. He took his case to the European Court of Human Rights at a later date, but by then Rampton was a law unto itself and he just caused himself more trouble. I often wonder how he was able to take the punishment he'd gone through.

One morning Ronnie, who was on D3 with me, informed me that he had been told to fix me; I was going to be kicked down three flights of stairs to D1. However, he had refused to take part knowing that if I got badly hurt, as he put it, he would be blamed. Besides, we had become quite good friends, and he felt I had had enough boot. At 10.35 I was called to do the back stairs. I knew what was coming and every step was a real effort, but I was determined not to beg for mercy as I knew that this would only prolong the treatment I was in for, and then I would be completely finished.

I was scrubbing the small step at the top of the back stairs when Mr Vincent and Mr Samuels started booting me. My bucket was kicked over and I was asked why I had thrown my bucket at the staff, then given some boot and fist. I was pulled up by my hair and made to stand at the top of the stairs. 'Please God, no.' I was shaking from top to bottom. I was told to put my head on my hand, Mr Samuels put one boot behind my feet, and I closed my eyes. Mr Vincent kicked me in the lower part of my stomach. I woke up in a heap at the bottom of the first lot of stairs, wet through. 'Come on, you bastard, we're not finished with you yet.' At that moment Mr Vincent was called away and Mr Samuels told me to get upstairs and start scrubbing again. As soon as I did so, I got some more boot, and curled up in a corner and covered my face. Mr Vincent came back. 'Go to the storeman and get tidied up, and remember, if anyone asks what's wrong, you fell over your bucket.'

Later that day I was interviewed by a doctor about the reasons I was in Rampton, and put on tablets which would stop my sex drive. I wasn't asked about the state I was in. I was put back on scrubbing out the toilets and Ronnie slipped me in a drink of tea and a roll-up.

Next day I went into the office and told Charge Nurse Thompson that my back was very painful. I said I must have hurt it when I fell over on the stairs the day before. He gave me some wintergreen to rub into my back, and allowed me to sit in the dayroom all day. If I had told him how it had really happened I would probably have been taken to D1 for making a false statement about staff, although everyone on the ward must have known what had taken place by now. I knew I could take very little more, so the next morning I went to the office before breakfast and confronted Mr Groves. 'Let's forget rank and go to a side room and fight man to man.' I knew I stood no chance of winning, but at least I would die like a man. He told me to start scrubbing the toilets out — with my back it was hell. I was then called into the office while the rest were having breakfast. To my utter amazement, I was told I had a man's body and a child's mind, and if I caused any more trouble on the ward, I would go to D1.

I never received any more boot or fist treatment on the back stairs, thank God.

* * *

About this time I was accused of writing letters to the Ministry of Health complaining about staff. While I had every reason to do this, it was the last thing on my mind as there was little point. The only way to survive in the Rampton system, as it was then, was to complain about the top officials as Rampton was becoming a law unto itself with no holds barred. Once I had proved that all I wanted was to change my RMO, I was left alone. Nonetheless I had a shrewd suspicion that my letters to the National Council for Civil Liberties weren't being sent because I never received any replies, which was most unusual.

My first interview with a Ministry official took place in Mr Stewart's office with the deputy chief male nurse present. Dr Curtis was the Ministry interviewer at this time, and I soon learned that he had a lot of power and that patients who saw him could be sure of a fair and just outcome. Not long afterwards I was sent to see a Dr Ogilvy who told me he was my new RMO. I had got what I wanted. It had taken six months but I had got rid of Dr Saunders. However, he was to have the last laugh.

Dr Ogilvy took me off the horrible tablets I had been given, but not before they had left their mark. Since starting on the tablets my lips had got bigger and were very noticeable; I became very self-conscious about them.

* * *

I had lost Tom, my family hopes were now over and I'd lost what few friends I had. There was no hope of getting out, even if I ever felt I was fit to be released. There was no church to go into for comfort. My low periods were getting worse. I felt I had to do something to stop myself becoming a cabbage, so I decided to keep a diary and get some premium bonds which would give me some interest both daily and weekly. This worked for a while, but I found I needed something more. By luck I was asked to become storeman and kitchen man which meant I would be working all hours of the day and night. I hoped that this would give me no time to get low, and I worked and worked. There were always jobs to be done — I even started sewing clothing which should have been done in the sewing room.

* * *

Just after Christmas 1968, D3 was moved lock, stock and barrel into C3 so that D3 could be turned into an oddment ward. The DHSS (as the Ministry of Health was now known) had decided in its wisdom that Rampton, Broadmoor and Moss Side should have mixed types of inmates. Until that time, mentally ill people had always been sent to Broadmoor, and younger people, including sex offenders and people on hospital orders made on social grounds, had gone to Moss Side. Rampton had always taken anyone and everyone: it was a dumping ground for people who didn't fit into prison, a local hospital, local authority provision or the other two special hospitals. Now Rampton was receiving mentally ill people from Broadmoor and through the courts as well, hence the shake-up on D3.

56

I was moved back onto D3 the next morning and by midday patients from most of the other block wards were moved in too. They were of all age groups and types and — more importantly — grades. With the exception of D1, mixing patients like this was unheard of before in Rampton. The two charges and staff nurses who were posted on D3 were as different as apples and pears, which seemed to me to be another odd move. However, both charges had one very good point in common: they didn't allow any booting. Even charges like these take holidays though, and while the cat's away the mice will play.

Mike came up to D3 from E1, and within a week he'd made himself unpopular amongst the staff because he knew what his rights were, and let staff know that he knew. I was sitting in the storeroom one day sewing clothing and doing jobs in general when I heard the acting charge and staff nurses talking about Mike and how they were going to fix him. They arranged that the staff nurse would give Mike extra work after tea whilst everyone else was in the dayroom. He would be told to scrub the toilets out, while the staff nurse stood over him. Everything went to plan, and while Mike was scrubbing the toilets, you could hear the staff nurse shouting his head off at him. The charge nurse then came down to see what the problem was — exactly as they had arranged.

I decided to make supper, and shouted 'Supper's up' just as the charge entered the toilets. That way most of the other patients could (and did) see the aggro Mike was getting from the charge and staff nurses, so when he complained to his family there would at least be some witnesses to the act.

When the charge arrived, everyone was told to go back into the dayroom. The corridor was cleared and the charge and staff nurses kicked Mike along the whole length of the corridor to the office where the charge rang down to D1. Mike was bleeding from the mouth when I saw the two nurses taking him to D1. The next morning the regular charge nurse came on duty, and he was livid. He did not allow this sort of behaviour himself, yet he would still have to deal with the matter.

About 11.00 that morning the doctor who was Mike's legal representative in these matters interviewed quite a number of patients about the incident. However, most who had seen what happened either denied seeing anything, or avoided telling the truth. This was done out of fear, as they all knew that if they said anything, their lives would be made even more of a hell than they were already. Even I didn't tell the complete truth at this stage; the only time I felt I *could* help Mike was when the police were brought in, as I felt sure would happen in this case. However, by the time the police came on the scene, two patients who had made unwritten statements to the doctor had been moved off the ward and given their villa and privileges, one had been recommended for discharge, and the others had been frightened off. When the police did eventually get round to doing their interviews, there was no case left to answer.

* * *

It was while I was on D3 that I came across one of the most despicable people I am ever likely to meet in my life. Mr Bryant had absolutely no respect for his fellow human beings, whether staff or patients, and he wasn't happy unless he kicked at least one patient a day. He even played staff off against each other, solely in the hope of gaining a higher post, and in fact it was on such an occasion that I crossed swords with him.

D3 was running smoothly until he was posted to the ward. Within the first few days he began unsettling the charge and his deputy, and by the end of the month there was open hostility between them. The situation got so bad that both the charge nurse and the staff nurse were sent to see the senior nursing officer, and everyone on the ward was suffering. The patients of course were getting the rough end of the stick because while the charge and the staff nurse were in open conflict, Bryant was using the situation to do what he liked, booting and hitting patients, putting them in locked rooms and giving them the needle.

However, every dog has its day, and I decided it might be mine. Being kitchen and storeman in Rampton is like being a red band in prison. You are in a position of trust, which is very hard to earn but so easy to lose. In order to survive you have to become a diplomat which means showing equal loyalty to staff and patients. At times this can be very difficult because neither side really trusts you. Weighing up the odds, I did what every rule at Rampton forbids both staff and patients to do in this sort of situation. I decided that because of my unsteady position and the trust placed in me, my first loyalty must be to the regular charge of each shift, then to my fellow patients, then to the rest of the staff. When the staff nurse went off duty, I asked the charge nurse if I could have a private word with him. I closed the office door because I was afraid, and I still wasn't sure I was doing the right thing. I then told the charge that I had seen Mr Bryant set himself up against the staff nurse and use the situation to his own advantage. By the charge's reaction, I knew he understood what I was doing and why. I was sent out of the office feeling that I'd been given a flea in my ear, and a silent thank you at the same time. When the shifts changed, I did the same with the staff nurse who was acting charge, and the same thing happened.

In the next monthly list of staff postings, Bryant was moved to a different unit, and D3 became a smooth-running ward again. Internal politics in Rampton are so complicated I could write a book on that subject alone.

STRUGGLE FOR POWER

By the late 1960s, Rampton was becoming more and more unsettled: staff were in open conflict. Mr Platt took over from Mr Stewart with a new title, principal nursing officer. He had been at Rampton for over twenty years, and most of that time had been on the therapy side. He and Dr Rolands teamed up well and started to implement changes for the benefit of patients. These changes were bound to be unpopular, but they were necessary if Rampton was to move forwards rather than backwards. First though the faceless bureaucrats had to enforce the recommendations of the Salmon Report.

The Salmon Report set out the findings of a government committee which looked into the role of the health service from the Ministry down to the smallest hospital. This committee suggested that Rampton should be divided into units, rather than being run as one big hospital. Each unit would be run by a nursing officer who would have a given number of staff. All nurses on the same unit would be number-graded so that there was a chain of command and responsibility — which there has to be if there is a large number of people working together. Under this system the unit nursing officer or the senior nursing officer can make a decision on the spot if there is a disagreement on the ward rather than waiting two or three days for the matter to be sorted out elsewhere.

The power struggle which went on behind the scenes was amazing. Dr Rolands and Mr Platt implemented a system where each unit had its own responsible medical officer, medical officer and nurses number 9, 7, 6 and 5 (the principal nursing officer was number 10). Nurses numbered 1 to 5 were staff just starting out in the profession and junior staff nurses. All appointments were made internally; the new number 7s were taken from amongst the charge nurses which meant that new charge nurses had to be appointed from the ranks of the staff nurses, and some junior staff would get their first postings. New staff coming into Rampton have to start off in the junior posts, no matter what stage they've reached in their career. This system was one of the major causes of unrest and mistrust between staff, and needless to say the patients were caught in the middle. Patients were treated so unfairly that they became very unsettled, and the rate of escapes went up by 100 per cent. The unions at Rampton and the press made out that this was the fault of Dr Rolands and Mr Platt, but in my opinion blame should fall squarely on the shoulders of the nursing staff numbers 1-8. Dr Rolands and Mr Platt implemented the Salmon Report and introduced reforms which meant that patients were treated in a much more human way. It was a masterpiece of work.

*   *   *

While the whole system was being overhauled, more and more people were being transferred from Broadmoor to Rampton. While at Broadmoor these patients had some rights. At Rampton they had none. It was no wonder that when they found themselves on D1 they also found themselves in hot water. In fact, quite a few patients who were transferred to Rampton from Broadmoor found themselves applying to be sent back.

Many of the people coming into Rampton were said to be psychopaths, a label which covers a wide range of behaviour with no set pattern. For example, one guy smashed a shop window when he was having family problems: he was labelled a psychopath and sent to Rampton. A lady who was arrested for shop-lifting refused to be locked in a cell in Holloway Prison with two murderers. She climbed the prison chimney in protest, and was labelled a psychopath. A guy was raped by an older man and in defending himself killed his attacker, quite by accident. He too was labelled a psychopath and sent to Rampton. The worst example I can recall is the case of a person who was so down and out that he stole a bottle of milk. For this he was labelled a psychopath and sent to Rampton where he has been for 30 years.

An institution run by ward and senior nursing staff with fear, mistrust and unjustness was hardly the ideal place to help these types of patients. Dr Rolands and Mr Platt were not receiving backing from either the Home Office or the Ministry of Health. Patients like myself realised what was going on and could foresee what was inevitable within a short time. Alone against this background Dr Rolands and Mr Platt brought in sweeping changes, such as the introduction of opportunities for male and female patients to mix, both in treatment and socially. For the first time in Rampton, school classes were mixed. Patients were allowed to wear their own clothes, and the weekly dance became a social occasion where male and female patients could sit at the same table and dance together without staff standing at different points down the middle of the floor. At last you could dance properly without fear of getting too close to your partner. Soft drinks and biscuits were also issued. Socials were arranged between male and female wards. Bingo sessions (at which I was after a year to become caller) were held on Wednesday nights. Evening classes were introduced, and visiting days were made more open and pleasant. Church services became mixed too. Dr Rolands and Mr Platt certainly altered the day-to-day existence of the patients, and it would have worked well had all the nursing staff had the welfare of patients at heart, as so often claimed in the media.

*   *   *

1972 was a year of private feuds and bitter conflict for power between staff and management. One of the nurses' unions was gaining power under leaders who knew everything there was to know about union rules, but nothing about nursing and less about man.

The DHSS (as the Ministry of Health was now called) had given Dr Rolands and Mr Platt the go-ahead to introduce a new staffing system which would give patients more work and social hours. Instead of spending 11½ hours a day in bed, we would spend only nine hours. The staff were to be offered two shift systems, plus staff roster, and generous grants were to be made. All these arrangements were open for discussion and suggestions for changes a good nine months before the new times and shifts were to be implemented.

On 1 October 1972 the new staff shifts came into force, and from this moment on the vast majority of staff showed their open dislike for the shifts and for the DHSS, the Home Office and the Rampton management. They used any number of tricks to get their own way in the matter.

They allowed patients to escape so that people would think that the other shift system was more secure.

They forced patients to write petitions.

They stopped all visits to patients.

They stopped patients working, and then claimed that the patients were backing them.

They stopped all patients' mail getting in and out.

When the press and TV crews arrived, they got patients to shout from the windows that staff should get what they wanted (in normal circumstances shouting wasn't allowed). In some cases the staff were standing behind the patients threatening them with boot and fist if they didn't shout.

They forced the patients to complain about management, especially about Dr Rolands and Mr Platt.

They caused trouble between patients in order to prove that the new day was too long for patients to be awake.

Why was there so much opposition to the new reforms? The answers are simple. One of the most important reasons went back to 1961 when the staff won their bid for a long day shift system (one day on/one day off). No way were the authorities going to allow a long day shift system, but the Ministry allowed the staff to make fools of Dr Rolands and Mr Stewart (then chief male nurse). The union threatened action and of course this undermined Dr Rolands and Mr Stewart's authority. The Ministry gave way to the young and militant staff, and this was the first time that the nurses' union got its own way without even trying.

Once the long day shift was implemented, 90 per cent of the staff got jobs on their days off (I heard it said that there were a lot of fiddles with these spare time jobs). With so many married couples working at Rampton, this system was ideal: at important times of the day, like before and after school, there was always someone at home. The split shift system introduced in 1972 meant that a lot of staff would either lose out on their spare time jobs or on overtime.

There was yet another reason for staff hostility to the new system. Giving patients a long day up with more work and social life meant that staff had a lot more duties to perform. This did not go down well at all — even before the new shift system started, staff always complained about being on this or that duty. Patients such as myself officiated at the bingo and dances because staff insisted that these were not nursing duties, and refused to take part.

It was during this period that I came across the most blatant misuse of patients' rations I ever encountered. I was by then in Beeches Villa where we had a choice of menu for dinner and tea. As storeman and kitchen man I was detailed to make the menu list out and help serve the food. On one particular teatime when I had ordered enough for twelve ham salads, a nurse came into the kitchen and told me that he was having a party that night. He then took all the salad except the lettuce for his party! I had twelve meals to find from somewhere, so I asked the charge nurse to ring the main kitchen for food for twelve patients: I had to make out that I'd dropped the main course. Had it been any other time I would have reported it to the charge, but with the situation as it was I would have been in big trouble and would probably have been accused of causing more friction between staff and patients.

The split shift system did not last more than a month, and as always the patients suffered. In the long term the DHSS and the Home Office's stupidity spelt the beginning of the end of any good Rampton could do for anyone, be they patient or staff.

* * *

Then came the final blow, a most appalling act which confirmed that Rampton was a law unto itself, as it is today, beyond the control of the Home Office and the DHSS. The majority of Rampton staff demanded the sacking of Dr Rolands and Mr Platt, their excuse being that these two men were responsible for the unrest and trouble in the hospital. Unbelievably, they got their way. Even a patient like myself had to wonder in disbelief at this decision. We knew as well as they did that the staff would now rule Rampton in their own way, and we all knew what this meant.

In my opinion, Dr Rolands worked wonders at Rampton and never received the acclaim he justly deserved. I wrote to him saying that I was sorry to see him leave, although I had not always agreed with what he said about me, and that I hoped he would be treated a lot better in his next appointment. Little did I know that he had not been offered another appointment at this time. But for the fact that an ex-Rampton doctor was by then in charge of Moss Side Hospital, and got Dr Rolands a position as a RMO (a post a lot junior to his position at Rampton), this good man might still not be doing the sort of job he had devoted his life to.

I wrote to the DHSS complaining, as usual, but with no joy. Since Dr Curtis had stopped visiting Rampton, it was a waste of time complaining to the DHSS; the official interviewers were indifferent to any complaints patients made about medical or nursing staff.

* * *

Dr Hunter took over from Dr Rolands, and Mr McKenzie took over from Mr Platt. In my opinion, Mr McKenzie was the wrong man for the job; although he was principal nursing officer he didn't command the authority this position held. Dr Hunter was totally different from Dr Rolands in that he called a spade a spade. He must have known that if he tried to bring in major changes he would have trouble on his hands and that he could expect little or no backing from the DHSS. However, he *did* implement changes, and he did it in such a way that the staff had no choice but to accept them. The introduction of social workers is a good illustration of Dr Hunter's reforms. Until that point there had been one welfare officer to deal with the problems of 1,000 patients. Mrs Martin was leaving, having done an excellent job considering the workload she had. Dr Hunter brought in social workers (new name, but same job), and assigned a number of them to each unit.

Dr Hunter was also medical superintendent for Balderton Hospital. Eastdale, a rehabilitation unit for patients from Rampton and Moss Side, had just been built in the grounds at Balderton, and Dr Hunter interviewed all the patients who were to be allocated a place at Eastdale. Staff had their say, but Dr Hunter didn't allow them to dictate who went to the unit and who didn't.

* * *

Dr Rolands, Mr Platt and then Dr Hunter introduced many changes. Some of the major reforms are still in force, but others have disappeared. This is bound to happen when people who are really dedicated are either dismissed, or leave.

RAMPTON LIFE

Only patients and staff can really understand Rampton of course, but these glimpses of daily life at the hospital might give you a better insight into what went on — and into some of Rampton's unwritten rules.

*　*　*

Each villa is situated in the middle of its own grounds, all wired off, and there is a big walled square at the end of blocks C, D and E. 'Court time', as it was known, happened every day; staff and patients from the blocks and villas would go outside and, depending on the weather and who was in charge, we would walk about, play football or just sit around. At weekends everyone would go on to the big KG field. Before it was turned into a sports field, it was the hospital's kitchen garden, hence the name KG.

Each year there was a sports day where each ward would get points for the usual events. The ward with the most points would receive the sports cup, and individual winners would get a money slip to spend at the patients' shop. I'll never forget my first sports day back in 1959 — it was quite an eye-opener. The male patients sat to the left of the field, the female patients sat on the right and, to my amazement, a group of young children were seated on the far side. I knew there were a few, but not this many. All around the outer field staff sat in twos and threes. Apart from patients and staff in D1, the rest of Rampton was on the field. I never knew so many people could gather together in one place.

*　*　*

In one of my many private discussions with the Rev Hewitt, I told him I would like to start a patients' magazine. He said that if I wrote to the Ministry and gained permission, he would give me all the help I needed, so I wrote that week to the Ministry and to my RMO, Dr Ogilvy. Dr Ogilvy said he would back the idea, and within a month permission was granted by the Ministry — against the wishes of ward and administrative staff.

Setting up the *Rampton Reveille* was quite a hard task. I knew that Carstairs Special Hospital in Scotland had a magazine which had been running for some time with great success, and that Broadmoor also published a newspaper. I wrote to the Carstairs editor for advice, and Dr Ogilvy got in touch with the Broadmoor editor; both were very helpful. The Rev Hewitt, who was to be our legal adviser, agreed to arrange the necessary equipment, and I relied on him to get the female patients involved in the magazine. I had little to do with the women myself, but both sides needed equal cover if the paper was to have an impact throughout Rampton.

From the very beginning I was determined to run the *Rampton Reveille* on a straight line. I wanted it to be neither anti-authority nor pro-authority, and hoped it would give patients a say on any subject they wished to write about. I had to find the right sort of patients to be on the editorial committee, but when I submitted my list to the Rampton management, it didn't go down too well — as I'd expected. For the sake of getting the magazine off the ground, I had to accept a compromise as to the membership of the editorial committee. Equipmentwise, we were allocated the grand total of two typewriters, a dozen pens and pencils, half a dozen scribbling pads and duplicating stencils, and two staplers. We were allowed to meet once a week for three hours, and the duplicating had to be done by Rev Hewitt on the main office machine. Despite these handicaps, the magazine started off well. Patients were buying copies at 3p each, and at one point we could have sold more than we were printing.

From the beginning I took control by chairing the editorial committee and editing the magazine. However, when Rob came to join us I worked it so that he took over the chairmanship. Rob and I were of the same opinion on how the magazine should be run, but because of one or two controversial articles about the relationship between patients and staff and patients' requests for changes, the committee started voting against more and more articles that Rob and I wanted to publish. The complaints about the magazine and myself became so bad that it was affecting the sales of the *Reveille*, so I resigned. It was interesting to note that shortly after I resigned the magazine became a ward newspaper rather than a general magazine, and published hospital news rather than views.

*　*　*

Needing outlets to give me an interest in the outside world, I started doing the football pools so that each week I had something to look forward to when the results were published in the newspapers. I didn't buy my own newspapers because they were always censored before we could read them: pages or articles would be cut out if the authorities found something they thought unsuitable for us to read, for instance anything to do with the staff or patients' rights.

By the 1970s I was studying for my referee qualification, which was quite odd really as when Ken Stokes came to give a talk on football in the early 60s and I asked the Rampton authorities if I could become a referee, I nearly got into serious trouble! Very few people, staff *or* patients, thought I stood a chance of qualifying, and I must say that while the interest was there and I knew I would pass on the theory, I had my doubts about the practical side of refereeing. Mr Daley, a charge nurse who is a Grade 1 referee, took 12 of us on study classes and got the OK for us to referee and line patients' matches at weekends. The help he gave us was worthwhile, and nine of us — me included — passed the referee exam, which I think is a jolly good show. I received a very high mark, and I felt so proud for myself and for Mr Daley and the rest of the class. It also helped me build up my confidence for the practical side of refereeing.

Refereeing a football match, which I started doing in 1976, is a most challenging and rewarding occupation. I say challenging, because although there is a set of rules laid down, each game is different, and you can never stop learning. It's rewarding in the sense that no matter what marks you receive (each team manager gives the referee marks from 0 to 10 at the end of the match), you know when you've had a good game, and you feel proud to have taken part in this sport.

Only once did I ever feel like giving up refereeing, and that was just before I came out of Rampton. After I qualified, I refereed a few league matches and lined a lot more, and at Christmas 1976 I was asked to referee a staff/patients match. I agreed for two reasons. Firstly I felt that the fact that I was asked indicated that people believed I could handle a needle match like this. Secondly, I felt it was better to test myself *now* rather than when I got out on the circuit.

My first mistake was to go out on the pitch with the preconceived idea that I would play a low key role. Knowing this to be a needle match, I should have asserted my authority from the dressing rooms onwards. However, my worst mistake was to allow some of the staff to intimidate me. I promised myself that I would never officiate at football again in Rampton unless I was allowed to have all the powers accorded to referees in the rules set out by the Football Association.

No matter what level of football is involved, I look at it only from the point of view of the sportsman and the set of rules laid down by the sporting body. Come the day a referee sees it as a business and doesn't enjoy going out in all weathers, he should pack up his boots!

*   *   *

Needless to say, patients become ill from time to time, and I had a particularly bad episode while I was on D3. I started being sick first thing in the morning and towards the end of the day; I was dizzy and I had odd pains in my stomach. I also started getting bouts of asthma which were mainly psychosomatic. I was put under sedation when I got a bad attack, but otherwise I just had tablets three times a day and at night, which was a help. For weeks I had this sickness and pain along with the dizzy spells, and they got worse every day. The charge nurse kept sending me to see the medical officer who just told me to rest. Some days they moved me to E1 for a while. By now most of the staff had realised it was a rumbling appendix, but not my good friend the medical officer.

For the first week in May that year I was in and out of E1 like a yo-yo. Things came to a head in the early hours of one Friday morning. I felt so terrible that I rang the alarm bell. The night chief took me down to D1 and got in touch with the duty medical officer, who just happened to be the doctor who had been seeing me all week. Lo and behold, he ordered me to have an enema, and the next thing I remember is waking up the following morning in the side room on E1 with the doctor standing over me. He asked me if I was OK, and I said 'Yes Sir'. He then said I could go back to my own ward. I took four steps out of the room and felt terrible: how I got back to D3 I'll never know. I was going in and out of dizzy spells all Saturday, and when I awoke next morning it was as much as I could do to crawl from my bed to the office. I just wanted to die. I was put back to bed, and dozed off. Coming round, who should I see but the charge nurse and the so-called doctor who was supposed to be treating me. I couldn't make out all of what they were saying but I did hear the doctor say very clearly: 'He can't go to hospital today. It's Sunday'. I couldn't believe it. Some time later the charge brought in the medical superintendent, and I overheard him say: 'I will not interfere with another doctor's patient, but I suggest you get the doctor down here now to get his man into hospital'.

Sometime on Sunday afternoon I went to Worksop Hospital by ambulance, and that is all I remember until the Monday. On that day I heard the two staff escorts saying that Rampton wanted me back immediately but the doctors at Worksop wouldn't allow me to be moved.

I spent nearly two weeks at Worksop, and when I got back to Rampton I was seen by a doctor every day for another two weeks. I was transferred back to D3 after three weeks' rest.

*   *   *

'Bonehead', the nickname bestowed on me by Mr Stewart, eventually faded, and was replaced by another — 'Dr Rowlands'. They called me this because I always tried to look neat and tidy. I wore casual clothing such as a sports jacket and neatly-pressed trousers, plus a clean collar and tie, on the ward, and changed into a suit whenever I went off the ward.

One Christmas I decided to send for some new clothes through a catalogue, this being the only way for patients in Rampton to purchase new things. I posted off my exact measurements for a suit, plus the full amount of money, thinking that it would be quite a simple job to get my order sent to me. However, much to my surprise, it was more trouble than it was worth. The order came through after a month and the suit was far too small, so I sent it back. After another month, another suit arrived, but this time in the wrong material and still too small. On top of all this the mail order company charged me for both suits! I returned the second suit and said I wanted my money back. It took me *two years* to get my money back, during which time I was threatened by a debt collector who reckoned that I owed money for one suit because I'd purchased two. I was also blacklisted by the company. Eventually I got my way after writing to the chief constable at Nottingham, but I wonder if it would have happened if I hadn't been in Rampton.

* * *

These days patients in Rampton are paid on a weekly basis, and are able to visit the shops once a month to buy whatever they want — all so different from when I first went to Rampton. In the old days, patients were paid according to the ward they were on, and the work they did. For example, a new patient would start off with 5s (25p), and you could work your way up to the top job (the staff club job) which paid £1.17s 6d (£1.88) a week. Of course patients never handled cash! We would be given a sheet of paper to write out our rex list (shopping list) once a month, and that was that.

This system worked well for two very good reasons. Firstly, from the moment a patient went into Rampton he had to prove that he could be trusted. Once you had earned your trust, whether wardwise or jobwise, you got paid accordingly. Secondly, there was a set pattern of payment which couldn't be changed without Mr Stewart's permission. Even if you were to be punished in some way, no-one could interfere with your money — which is more than could be said for the new system.

In the 1970s, the Rampton psychologist introduced a new system which worked like this. Each day every patient could earn a maximum of four points for work, behaviour and cleanliness. These points represented money, so in theory patients would try that bit harder at work and smarten themselves up to earn more points. However, it didn't work like that in practice. If a staff had something against you, he naturally marked you down; the new system was totally unfair and open to all sorts of abuses. Although a patient could in theory earn up to £5.00 a week, the average pay-out was usually about £3.00 — of which £1.50 was money due to the patient as of right. Such a system could never work properly in an environment like Rampton.

* * *

The most persistent feature of Rampton life was the violence; I had my share and I saw a lot more. When I was bingo calling, for example, I once saw one of the female patients hit a female nurse, and what followed left a bad taste in my mouth. Some male and female nurses got hold of the girl and kicked hell out of her on the corridor. The screams were terrible. Back on the ward I heard one of the male staff say: 'We fixed the bastard cow. I enjoyed that bit of fun'. I just ignored these remarks as you either become immune to remarks and violence such as this after a while, or it

66

affects you so much that you feel really ill. The pitiful part about it is that there's really no need for it.

The best incident to prove this point took place on Beeches Villa. A staff nurse was standing by the back door which was open because two patients were going to clean the yard. Without warning Roy started screaming and ran through the door with the yard brush, knocking the nurse out cold as he went. Another nurse was on his way in to take a patient to hospital, and Roy ran screaming at him and broke his nose in two places. That left Mr Piper on his own. He tried to talk Roy down, but Roy got hold of his tie, pulling him to the ground and hurting his back. While this was going on, I was standing at the kitchen door which had been left open in the confusion. Seeing Mr Piper in trouble, I shouted to a staff nurse walking into the next villa, but got little response. I assumed he hadn't heard me, so I got hold of Roy. However, I had to let him go as I was doing more harm than good — the more force I used to pull him off, the more discomfort Mr Piper must have felt. I changed tactics and got hold of Roy in between his legs, giving him a quick squeeze. He let go of Mr Piper for a few seconds, which gave me time to grab hold of his feet while Mr Piper got hold of his arms. We pinned him down until Mr Piper had calmed him down a little. I then let go of his feet and we got him inside, but while we were taking him upstairs he started screaming again. Mr Piper was pushed against a wall, and I slipped and let go for a few minutes. We eventually got him into a room, locking the door quickly. The staff nurse who had his nose broken had by this time phoned for help. Two chiefs and two charge nurses came within a few minutes, followed by a doctor, then some other staff, and Roy was escorted to D1.

In a few minutes of madness Roy had attacked three staff, yet not once did he get any fist or boot treatment. He was handled with all the understanding he needed, and with the minimum of force, which proves that Rampton *can* cope with dangerous patients without the violence which exists on a day-to-day basis.

HAWTHORNE VILLA

One of the best-known characters in Rampton was Steve, a lad who was classified as insane. Accents were his party-piece; he could be a Scotsman, an Irishman or an Englishman, and if he was in the right mood he could be very funny. Most staff took it for granted that he was simple and mad, and he would play on this — what he could get away with was no-one's business. One day on D3 corridor he pulled up his RMO and asked for his villa, as he'd done many times before. The RMO turned to the charge nurse and said: 'Do you know, this is the only man I know who is totally insane with a sense of humour. Give him any villa he wants, then I'll get some peace'. I was sitting in the ward storeroom while this was going on, and I burst out laughing. The RMO put me on extra work, but the charge nurse overlooked this as I'm sure he saw the funny side too.

* * *

Not everyone got their villa privileges as easily as Steve of course. I got mine after five years in Rampton. I was transferred to Hawthorne Villa as a ward worker: Hawthorne is mainly for severely mentally handicapped patients, so there have to be a few ward workers to look after the other patients and to keep the ward clean. I was very pleased to be offered my villa but I got a nasty shock the morning I arrived on Hawthorne. Of all the rotten luck in the world, Mr Bryant was there — the man who had caused so much conflict between staff and patients on D3. He knew that I had talked to the other staff about him on D3 so there was no love lost between us. He made it quite plain that he would see me in detention the first chance he got.

I was put on cleaning the toilets while Mr Bryant went through all my belongings. I had foreseen what he would do, so I kept my diaries in my pocket. I knew that if these yearly accounts ever got into the hands of the staff, my life wouldn't be worth living. They contained a day-to-day record of beatings, with dates and times of every incident I'd witnessed between staff and patients, as well as notes on my own doings — interviews with doctors and staff, ways of using the system and so on. These diaries had enough information in them to have me sent down to D1 for the rest of my life — which I feared would have been short.

The next day the regular charge nurse came on and I was taken off cleaning the toilets and given a different job.

* * *

Being in a strange villa was most unsettling. While I'd wanted to move, I'd somehow got attached to D3 and I went through a low period again. I was foolish to let myself get in this state because it led to my first bad mistake in Rampton. I left my locker and case open and one of the patients got hold of my diaries. Fortunately he had the sense to see that he could make something out of them by selling them back to me. There was very little I could do except play ball, and when I did eventually get them back (by a stroke of luck), I destroyed them in fear. Of course now I wish I hadn't because the information would have been invaluable for this book.

Where there's a will, there's a way, and I didn't last long in Hawthorne Villa. Bryant, via another patient, accused me of stating that the unit nursing officer was eating meals on the ward. By the time these remarks had got back to the officer, they'd become a completely different — and much worse — story. The set-up nearly worked: the unit officer, knowing little about me and being outraged (which he had every right to be), had to act on what he had been told by another member of staff. By this time I was a nervous wreck; I couldn't eat because the suspense was terrible. This went on for four days, and I was dying to get it all over with as soon as possible. It may seem a bit silly to get worked up over something like this, but in Rampton an incident far less important would have been enough to cause those involved to be struck with fear. Being innocent was worse because I knew that no matter what *I* said, whatever a member of staff said would be taken as gospel, even if it was a lie. It was a perfect opportunity for the many people who already had it in for me, and I was within a gnat's whisker of being sent down to D1. Dr Saunders, Dr Rolands and others were brought in on the matter, and in the end I was transferred to the male hospital block. All this happened while the charge nurse was acting number 7 on another ward. When I did eventually see him I asked to be moved back, and he agreed. I wasn't going to stay on the hospital block for long if I could help it. It was so depressing, and anyway I was being unjustly punished for something I hadn't done.

* * *

Patients were subjected to a surprising amount of ill-treatment in the villa area, and not just boot and fist. Mental cruelty is in some ways far worse than physical punishment.

THE WAY OUT

I hadn't been in Rampton very long when I first applied for a Mental Health Review Tribunal hearing. I was aware that there wasn't much chance of getting out, and I knew I was nowhere near ready. This costly exercise was solely to find out what was being put on my file and to get used to being interviewed by outsiders. To hear someone call me Mr Harding instead of Harding made me feel like a human being again.

★   ★   ★

In 1971 my social worker told me to put in for another tribunal, and encouraged me to apply with the intention of gaining my transfer from Rampton rather than just doing it to see how I was getting on. I made the application, and my RMO came to see me, which is usual when a patient puts in a request for a tribunal. He told me that he didn't know how I could apply for a tribunal for another ten years. I referred this remark back to my social worker and to the DHSS, to be told by the Department that I was entitled to a tribunal once every two years, and was well overdue. My social worker told me to go through with it, and even got me a solicitor to help me put my case at the hearing. Given that my RMO would be against my transfer, however, the solicitor was bound to ask a certain number 8 if his client was fit to be released, and the outcome of the tribunal was not unforeseen.

I wasn't to be discharged, and in a way I wasn't sorry: I wasn't convinced in myself that I was ready to go. For the last few years I had been so concerned with internal politics and with keeping my head above water, so to speak, that I hadn't taken a good hard look at myself and my past for some time. Had it not been for two newspaper articles, I might never have started to think of looking after my own interests and coming to terms with myself.

When I took complete responsibility for the crime and was sent to Rampton, my one fear was that if the second party got away with it, something similar might happen again. To my horror I read how a young lad was saved by an act of God from a terrible fate. My one-time partner was put away this time, and for his sake and the public's, I hope he never gets out. While he is to be pitied, he is rotten to the core.

The other article was about Trish, someone who will always be very special to me.

Trish was 5ft 7ins tall with short black hair, brown eyes and a fresh-looking face. She looked a lot

70

younger than she really was with her unmade-up face and small but nice body. I first saw her at the social dance, and each week I would sit and watch her dancing — sometimes with men but mostly with other girls.

I so much wanted to dance with her, just to hold her and talk to her. Weeks went by and I would sit just admiring her beauty. If only I could talk to her, but what would I say? I had never been with a girl before, and I was scared stiff of putting my foot in it. I would go back to D3 upset and sometimes ashamed. Here was the first girl that I'd ever felt for, and I couldn't even say hello. Had it been a boy there would have been no difficulty. 'Why?', I asked myself: 'It's unfair.' More weeks went by, and now and again our eyes would meet. I'd give her a nod and she would respond in an off-hand manner.

I decided to speak to Mark about it. He gave me a lot of useful advice, and one Saturday evening I got up as Trish came over and asked her for a dance. The woman dancing with her said no, but I got Neil to let me dance with his partner Kathy so I could worm my way nearer Trish. As luck would have it, Kathy was on the same ward as Trish, so I asked her to tell Trish that my name was Len and that I wanted to have just one dance with her, no strings attached.

The next week, after getting the OK from Kathy via Neil, I asked Trish for a dance. It was heavenly when she was in my arms. I probably talked too much because of nerves, but that didn't put her off me. Not only did I dance two dances with her that night, but she also said I could dance with her the following week as well. I shouted goodnight to her across the floor, and went back to the ward on cloud nine.

The next time we met I told her I'd started work in the printing shop. The printers overlooked the female occupational shops, and I would often see her through the window. I asked her if she needed anything, because the female patients get far less money than the men, but she said no. However, we agreed to make the most of the system, and arranged to meet on the corridor some mornings. I planned to give her some little gifts from the patients' shop.

At the weekly dance, you were likely to get kicked out by the staff if you got too close to your partner, but I chanced that. As long as Trish was around I didn't mind being in Rampton. My days were much happier as I knew I felt for her. It was a one-sided affair, but that didn't matter. For the first time in ages I had some excitement and could look forward to something which was nearer reality than buying premium bonds each week. Life was never so good.

Weeks, months, passed by. I was so happy, although I wasn't Trish's regular dancing partner, and I knew she didn't feel the same for me as I felt for her. Then came a devastating blow, although I suppose I should have foreseen it. Trish put in for a tribunal hearing and it was a foregone conclusion that she would get her discharge — you could always tell by the attitude of staff if someone was going to be released. I so much wanted Trish to get out of Rampton, yet I so much wanted her to be with me. Just before she left we met on the corridor, and our goodbye kiss will always remain in my thoughts. That day, when she went, I thought it would be the last I'd hear of her. I wish it had been.

Just after I found out about Tom, I read in the *News of the World* that Trish had been found in an old disused house pumped full of drugs. She was dead.

Trish deserved a lot better than that; she was so young, and she'd not had much of a life. A charge nurse told me that Trish had found the peace in Heaven she'd wanted so much on earth. I'm sure that God has blessed her with the peace of mind she so desperately needed.

*   *   *

After Trish's death, I promised myself I would never love again, and went back into my self-imposed solitude. No dances, no social life in or out of the ward: I could always find plenty of work in the kitchen and stores to keep me busy. I allowed myself some tobacco and chocolates, but the rest of my money I saved because I needed to believe that one day I would get out, and when that day came I would need all the money I could get to help me set up home again.

I so much wanted to believe that the time was right for me to leave and to find my place in society, yet I knew deep down that I wasn't ready. Having lived in an environment where there is so much violence, my main fear was that I didn't know how I'd react when I met violence in society. I needed more than anything to talk these matters over with someone, but I knew that if I stated how I felt and revealed how big a problem I had, I'd never get out. I therefore continued to keep myself busy so that I didn't have time to ponder or to let my feelings come to the surface.

Around this time I had yet another change of RMO, which meant going back to square one again — I wondered how many more times this was likely to happen. However, much to my amazement, my new RMO Dr Hassan was quite unlike any other doctor I had known all the time I had been in Rampton or Powick. He didn't ask me the usual questions, or make any quick or false promises. Neither did he dwell on my background in such a way that I felt I couldn't be totally honest with him. Because he didn't overwhelm me, he gave me the feeling that I was a somebody and not just a number and a case note. I'd spent so long in Rampton that I'd learned to mistrust and question everyone and think twice about everything. It was most unusual for me to have opened up and to have been so honest with this doctor, yet I felt so at ease with him and it was refreshing to unburden myself so freely.

I asked Dr Hassan for permission to work outside the confines of the villa, and he agreed — a welcome sign of his trust in me. The evening after we discussed this, however, Mr Foster, the senior nursing officer, called me into the office. 'While I'm in any form of authority you will get nowhere. I told you that when you first came back to Rampton.' He then told me that he had crossed out Dr Hassan's permission. I was shocked that he could overrule my RMO like that, and I complained bitterly. How could an office boy overrule a man who was legally responsible for my treatment? The next day I was interviewed by Dr Hassan again, and out of respect for him I didn't take the matter any further.

This incident proved to me that while the old school was running the place, Rampton could never go forward to become the leading hospital of its type, either in this country or abroad.

*　*　*

After being interviewed by Dr Hassan many many times, and going on a course with the Rampton psychologist over a period of two years, I was told by Dr Hassan that I was being considered for a transfer to the Eastdale Unit at Balderton Hospital. I had heard about Eastdale of course, but I wondered seriously whether I was ready to go and whether it was the right place for me. Much as I hated being at Rampton, I was not prepared to leave until I was sure in my own mind that I could fit into society and that society could accept me.

The first and most important step would be a case conference which would take two months to set up. This was to be attended by nursing and occupational staff, education and personnel officers, doctors and social workers — all the people who had dealings with me in Rampton. I would have to convince them that I was ready to leave: if I succeeded, I'd be on my way to Eastdale; if not, my transfer would be rejected.

At this time I first met Paul Goodman who was to be my new social worker. He seemed friendly enough, but I was more worried about him being on my case conference than I was about Dr Hunter who was in charge of the Eastdale Unit! However, after three or four meetings my worries about Paul (as I have come to call him) faded, and I knew he would give me a fair hearing.

Just before the case conference, I was interviewed by Dr Hunter — a magic name at Rampton. After nearly two hours' hard talking I felt drained mentally, but I knew that if I went to Eastdale I would be given the time I needed to adjust. If I felt uncertain about myself — as I did at that time — and went backwards instead of progressing, I would be returned to Rampton.

I decided to accept a transfer from Rampton to Eastdale if it was offered.

*　　*　　*

Twelve people sat in on the case conference and each had their own questions. It was a long and very deep-digging conference which went into the whole of my background and what I thought of my future. I was quite pleased when it was all over and I was able to leave. After a while I was called back in, and Dr Hunter told me that the conference would be recommending to the Home Office that I be transferred to Eastdale. This was just the beginning. Altogether I was interviewed by 21 people, not least Dr Greene from the Home Office, and had to wait for nearly three years from the first mention of a transfer until it actually took place. Had it not been for Dr Hunter and Dr Hassan, I'd have waited even longer.

While I was waiting to know whether the Home Office and the DHSS were going to agree my release, I was sent to Moss Rose Villa, which was then a pre-discharge ward. From here I was allowed occasionally to go shopping in Retford and Worksop with an escort. These trips into the outside world were so strange to me: I was so thankful to have a staff escort. I had money in my hand, but no regard to the fact that it might easily be stolen. Likewise I had absolutely no sense of danger in traffic. Time and time again I walked off the pavement into the road, unaware that I had done so because I was staring in amazement at all the shops and shoppers, plus of course the traffic seemed harmless enough to me. When I got back to Rampton I'd think: 'Christ, if I'm turned down now after tasting a little freedom, I think I'll turn my bags in'.

One Wednesday I returned to Moss Rose after bingo to find the charge nurse wanted to see me. He called me into the office and asked me how I was feeling. Then he smiled and told me that the number 7 would be coming to see me sometime that evening. I knew I had done nothing wrong, so this could mean only one thing. Sure enough, I was called to the office about half an hour later and told I would be transferred to Eastdale after three long years of waiting and uncertainty. Had I been turned down, I think I would have been relieved, but now I felt a mixture of relief, happiness and a little doubt. Relief that I knew a decision had been made, happiness at the thought of leaving Rampton for good, and doubts about the unknown to come.

*　　*　　*

The last two weeks at Rampton were awful. As much as I wanted to go, the thought of moving to a strange environment, and leaving the place I had made a sort of home, frightened me. I dreaded the idea of getting to know new people, but the most worrying thing of all was knowing that I would have to speak to women, as I had heard that there were female nurses at Eastdale. Apart from Trish, who is special as far as ladies are concerned, I had had no real social contact with women.

73

On Thursday 13 March 1977 I went to Eastdale with an escort of Rampton staff to have a look around. The reason they show you round at this stage is that you can still refuse to leave Rampton if you don't take to Eastdale. I was allowed to ask any questions I liked, and the acting charge nurse gave us a complete picture of Eastdale, which was most refreshing. In all the years I've spent in homes and hospitals and such places, I don't think I have ever been given a true insight into the system before moving in. I ran into Dr Hunter on my day in Eastdale: he stated that he was pleased I was at last coming to the unit. To my surprise, the people I met there were themselves. There was no 'act' put on. On my way back to Rampton I knew Eastdale was the ideal form of release for me. Whether I would be able to settle or adjust after so many years in Rampton, only time would tell.

5. THE BEGINNING OF A NEW LIFE

EASTDALE

Eastdale Unit, also known as Eastdale Villa, is a bungalow purpose-built for the rehabilitation of male patients from the four special hospitals which serve England and Wales — Rampton, Broadmoor, Moss Side and Park Lane. It was opened in 1974, and is the first of its kind in Britain. Although each Regional Health Authority was allocated £7.7 million to build and run such units, I believe that there are still only *two* in the whole of England.

Eastdale is situated in the main grounds of Balderton mental handicap hospital, and shares all the facilities and resources. It has 30 beds set out in two dormitories of eight beds and twelve single rooms. Apart from two rooms which have armoured-glass locked windows and locked doors, and the 'staff-assistance' telephone which is linked into the main hospital system, there are no obvious outward signs of security like bars on windows and locks on doors. Each person coming in to Eastdale is made aware that *any* anti-social behaviour will greatly increase his chances of being sent back where he came from.

The team of psychologists, nurses, teachers, technical training officers and social workers is hand-picked, and patients transferred to Eastdale from a special hospital can be assured that they will be treated in a just and fair manner, and as *individuals*, which is so important.

The word *rehabilitation* means just that at Eastdale, for everyone who comes to the unit starts a social training programme geared to his needs within a few days of admission. The daytime programme covers education and technical training (like learning a trade and getting used to working eight hours a day), and there is a small self-catering unit where patients are taught simple basic cooking and domestic management. The evening programme covers subjects such as personal relationships, aspects of growing up, the work of the Disablement Resettlement Officer, employment and unions, finance (building societies, post office and bank accounts), income tax, DHSS benefits, family planning, drugs, alcoholism, sex education, marriage guidance, communications, the police and public relations. Patients also attend social evenings and go on shopping trips (handling money for the first time in many years can cause problems). The idea is to encourage people to start thinking for themselves again, and to give them an insight into society which will help them resettle with confidence. The Eastdale staff take great pains to find out about the after-care services an individual will need. These services are brought in at an early stage so that the people involved get to know the patient well, which gives him every possible advantage when he eventually leaves Eastdale. Each person agrees with the full multi-disciplinary team the environment which will best suit him when he is discharged, be it a local hostel, a flat or his family home, and he is given the opportunity to familiarise himself with his new place on visits and weekend leave.

Every person going to Eastdale is given a reasonable amount of time to settle in and to begin the process of rehabilitation. However, there is only so much that can be done for someone; the rest he has to be able to do for himself. It was agreed before I went to Eastdale that I should spend a much longer period at the unit than is usual. Both my responsible medical officer at Rampton and Dr Hunter felt that because of the number of years I had spent in homes and hospitals, I had become very institutionalised. I had no confidence in myself and very little trust for anyone in authority. Most of this could be put down to the way one is treated in special hospitals, but I know that some of it was to do with my own failings.

As far as I am aware, 268 special hospital patients have been through Eastdale Unit, staying for periods from six to 14 months (the average stay being six to eight months). Two have been returned to the hospital they came from because there was no suitable accommodation for them in the community. Twenty-four are back in special hospitals for reasons which are in their own interest, and those of the public. That means 242 people who have come from special hospitals to Eastdale have been able to settle back into society in a way that meets their individual needs. No other government institution, be it a special hospital, prison, training centre or whatever, can claim this success. This proves the need for rehabilitation units like Eastdale, for no matter whether a person has been locked up for five or 25 years, he needs time to readjust to society, and it is in the interests of that individual and of the public at large that he should have an opportunity to make this adjustment.

I found the whole training programme at Eastdale invaluable, and without it I'm sure I would have been much less well-equipped to go into society. The only criticisms I have are really concerned with official policy, and not with the unit as such. One is that Eastdale doesn't cater for female patients: this is DHSS and Home Office policy, and is not the fault of staff. The other is that although there are 140 patients in the special hospital system waiting for a place at Eastdale, for the last 18 months only *nine* beds have been in use at any one time. This criminal situation is mostly due to the powers-that-be wanting to have the unit closed down.

★   ★   ★

Mr Floyd, the nursing officer, and a female nurse from Eastdale came to take me to the unit the week after my transfer was confirmed. Getting into the car outside Moss Rose Villa felt wonderful. I didn't believe it was really happening until I got out of the main gates of Rampton! I took one last look at Rampton, and thought this had got to be the beginning of a new life.

Arriving at Eastdale I felt quite unsettled. I had wanted so much to go to Eastdale, but I was afraid that I might not fit in, and there was still the same old hang-up about moving from one place to another whether I was in favour of the move or not.

For the first two weeks in Eastdale I went round in a state of disbelief. All the doors were left open and there were no bars on the windows — it seemed so odd to begin with, but what was most enjoyable was the little things like being able to have a cup of tea while watching television, just sitting around talking, or being able to watch a favourite programme or read in the evenings without being disturbed.

Lads who'd been on the unit for some time were different from how they were when I knew them in Rampton. This made me feel out of place until I realised that each had become a person in his own right, thinking and doing things for himself while remaining part of the unit. There was a comradeship based on friendliness and trust between the lads which I had never seen before. People tried to help each other, and it didn't matter if you were a newcomer or an old hand. The best way to explain the situation is to refer back to Rampton where a patient had to build a barrier between himself and other people — with patients and even more so with staff — and couldn't say what he really felt. At Eastdale the ex-patients were treated as people with their own personalities, and they and the staff spoke openly to each other. One could usually tell how long someone had been at Eastdale by the degree to which the barriers still existed between them and others. Of course, some people never drop the barriers, and in some respects this is understandable.

I took to Paul Goodman, the social worker, very quickly, because I had known him at Rampton: as far as I and many other patients were concerned, when he worked at Rampton he was not part of the system. However, making friends with the other staff on the ward was disturbing for quite a while. I would call them *Madam* or *Nurse*, and felt completely out of place in their company. The only staff I relaxed with and took to within a short time was Mr Attwell, the reason being that patients who had come back to Rampton had spoken very highly of him. When I arrived at Eastdale he came on duty that afternoon, and his presence on the unit seemed to create such a friendly atmosphere that I started calling him *Dad*, to a lot of people's amazement and some distaste.

During those first two weeks, I was given a thorough physical examination by the medical team, and saw the dentist. I was also interviewed by Mr Kerr, the training officer, who asked me what kind of work I was thinking of doing after my discharge and what I thought my capabilities were. Until that point I'd had no idea what I wanted to do *or* what my capabilities were — up to then they'd been of little importance. I filled in a form, and had a chat with Mr Kerr, which I found refreshing. Like all other members of staff, he called me *Mr Harding*, which sounded so out of place. In conversation with staff, I kept repeating 'Yes Sir' or 'Yes Madam', whichever the case might be — though on some occasions when a woman spoke to me I said 'Yes Sir' without thinking.

The more time I spent at Eastdale, the less institutionalised I became. However, this didn't come easily: whenever a doctor came into the room I would automatically stand up, drop whatever I was doing, and say 'Good morning or afternoon, Sir'. On one such occasion I was in the admin block while working with the porters at Balderton and Dr Hunter came in. I dropped the basket I was carrying, stood to attention, and called him Sir. In front of a good few people I was told quite bluntly that I was no longer in Rampton and should stop jumping to attention. This was the jolt I needed. I felt so embarrassed that from then on, except for the odd occasion when I wasn't thinking, I stopped what was an institutionalised reaction. More and more I became a person in my own right rather than a Burton's dummy.

The most important aspects of my rehabilitation started as soon as I arrived on the unit. Eastdale has certain set rules as all places must have, be they a closed environment or out in society, but apart from these I was *advised* and not *told* what to do. I therefore had to think for myself. I was to work an eight hour day in one of the training areas. In Rampton, unless you were a stores or kitchen worker, you only worked for about four hours. Once in Eastdale I had to train myself to have six to eight hours sleep a night instead of 11. This I found a big problem, and it took some time for me to adjust. The last, but not least, problem was getting used to handling money and carrying it around in your pocket — there was a great temptation to spend it. However, my middle name is Scrooge, and I had decided I wanted to own my own cafe, so I turned out to be quite good at saving money.

*　*　*

My first trip out of Eastdale was a ward outing to the Festival Hall in Nottingham. I was advised by the staff to be careful how much I drank as it had been roughly ten years since I had been out for a social evening. My favourite drink is cider, and of course it goes without saying that I had an enjoyable evening. It was said that I went round the car park saluting cars, but I don't believe that for one moment!

Such outings, which were called rehabilitating trips, were paid for from ward funds. Each lad put 80p of his weekly money into a kitty, and this paid for the coach, entrance fees and so on. The staff received no pay for taking us on these trips, and of course if there weren't enough staff able to go, the outing would have to be cancelled. Fortunately this only happened once in a blue moon, and the outing was always rearranged for a different date.

Every Saturday a staff out of uniform would take a group of those who hadn't been at Eastdale long enough to warrant day leave down to Newark for shopping, or out for a walk. These outings did me a lot of good as I felt fine — even safe if you like — while in the company of people I knew, but if I went into a shop on my own, no matter how many people were there I felt out of place and insecure. I can only put this down to having been in Rampton for so long. On one such outing, the escort caught me holding my hand out and letting the girl behind the counter take whatever money she required for what I had bought. I did this partly because I was not used to handling money, and partly because I was afraid of saying and doing the wrong thing. It wasn't unknown for me to call women Sir still, and it made me feel awful.

Until you're ready to go out on your own, you're always accompanied by staff (who allow you to call them by their first names when out of the hospital grounds). You then get your ground parole, followed by town parole and then full parole. At each stage, a case conference with Dr Hunter, nursing staff, a training officer and a social worker meets to discuss whether an individual should be given parole. Just because you've done the necessary time to gain your parole, it doesn't automatically follow that you'll receive it as of right. The interests of the public and of the person involved are taken into consideration, and quite rightly so.

After my first month at the unit I was allowed one ground parole; after three months' trial, town parole; and after four months, full parole. Each stage took me a little longer than most, as I needed more time to adjust.

I'll never forget my first long day parole, which was arranged for a Saturday from 8.30 am until 12.30 pm. I couldn't wait to get away on my own, so I was ready with my parole card dead on the dot of 8.30. I went out on my bicycle and did some shopping, which I was used to. By 9.00 am I'd bought everything I needed, so I started to wander around Newark. Then suddenly I stopped dead, looked around, and there was not one person I knew. I ran across the square, got on my bike and rode through two sets of red traffic lights and the wrong way up a one way street back to Eastdale. When I got there Dad was firm, but understanding, and made me realise that I'd panicked for no real reason. He repeated what he and others had been advising me: I had to go out and get used to being on my own.

From then on, I plucked up courage to go out alone. At first I just went into the village, but later as I gained confidence, I started going to Newark and staying out longer. I would often end up at *The Cock Inn,* a local public house, on my evening out. Going there was a good way of meeting people and getting used to people outside the unit, plus the landlord and his wife accepted us and treated us like any other members of the public although they knew what Eastdale was all about.

By the time the football season began, I was confident enough to go refereeing. I had refereed and lined matches for the Retford and District League while I was in Rampton, but I didn't know what to expect with the Nottinghamshire Football Association. I was an unknown quantity, and I knew very little about the players and club linesmen or the local pitches and equipment. What I got to know through my local referee association was very helpful, but although I had all the right know-how in theory, I still had to put this into practical use. My first few matches were indifferent, as my marking must have shown, but as the season went on I gained the self-confidence I needed to officiate properly. As I attended more and more local referees' meetings, and officiated at more and more matches — which I loved — I became part of the overall team. When all's said and done, that's what football is all about.

*　*　*

I hadn't formed a relationship with anyone for a long time because of the hurt over Trish, and when Dr Hassan in Rampton had suggested that I go on a course with a psychologist to sort out my mixed feelings towards people, I agreed. The course did me a lot of good, but even at Eastdale I really didn't know whether I would be able to form a normal relationship once I was out in a normal environment. Would I be able to converse socially so that I could form a relationship in the first place?

Having been in a male environment for about 34 out of my 35 years, and never having had any real interest in women apart from Trish, I had an awful emotional blockage. I felt inadequate and afraid of women, and had therefore built up a false impression which I had come to believe in. I told myself that a woman's place was in the home, and that any physical contact from kissing on the lips to intercourse was not allowed until after marriage. When a woman spoke to me it was 'Yes, Madam', 'No, Madam', and that was all. Of course I still needed to feel wanted and to have love and affection like everyone else; I wouldn't have been human if I didn't. I would get so lonely and depressed, and when I did form a relationship I would give all. In fact, with my relationships so far I'd given *too* much, which is why they'd ended up as a one way love and I'd taken so long to get over them.

After a few months at Eastdale, the old inner conflicts surfaced again. For perhaps the first time in my years in hospital, I made a close friendship without having any ulterior motive. The friendship was pure and clean, and it hurt me to think that some staff and fellow patients in the unit thought the worst about my intentions. I felt proud that at long last I could have a close friendship without there being an attachment of a sexual kind. It was a case of give a dog a bad name, and unknown to me I was just hours from being sent back to Rampton because of innuendoes and my own lack of insight into the situation.

Thank God the crisis passed, and in fact the other lad and I stayed friends until well after we had left the unit and gone our own way in society. However, I did without even realising it start something of that nature with a guy called Stuart, and this caused a lot of personal uncertainty for me.

While I was in Rampton, whenever I felt that my problems were getting me down I would involve myself in as much work as possible so there wasn't time to sit and brood. When I was transferred to Eastdale I was expected to do eight hours work a day to get me into the habit of working during the day and forming a social life for myself the rest of the time. So that I didn't have time to brood at Eastdale, I involved myself with the unit committees: I became the sports and entertainment organiser, then treasurer and finally chairman. As chairman, I had to set a good example: I wanted to be worthy of the trust Dr Hunter, Dad and Paul had placed in me, plus there were many people at Balderton who were against Eastdale and would use any bit of gossip or the slightest incident to further their cause to have the unit closed down and turned into a geriatric ward. Just as important, I felt I ought to form a normal sexual relationship with a woman. The *last* thing I wanted at this stage was to start another homosexual relationship.

I had seen Stuart in Rampton and had spoken to him on the odd occasion. When he first came to Eastdale it never occurred to me that I might later look towards him with affection, as I didn't particularly like him at first. We eventually became friends, although we were as different as apples and pears. I wanted to spend more and more time in Stuart's company, which he didn't seem to mind, but then came the moment we both knew would happen, a moment we hadn't discussed or arranged in any way. We had been close to this moment before, but we'd pulled away from it, partly through fear, and partly because our friendship would alter.

Stuart and I had one moment of togetherness, and I became so hung-up about it that it affected my behaviour. It was suggested that I would benefit from having one-to-one therapy with a psychologist. The Eastdale psychologist was a woman, and I didn't particularly like discussing my problems with her, partly because she was female, and partly due to the fact that I mistrust psychologists anyway. However, I knew that it was in my own interests to sort out my problems while I was at Eastdale — after all Rampton had failed to help me — so I opened up to the psychologist as quickly as my conscience would allow.

While I was having one-to-one therapy with the psychologist, I started to go to Nottingham in order to get used to being out on my own and spending the full day in a city. I decided to use the opportunity to find out whether I could have sex with a woman, so one Saturday I went looking for the sort of public house where I could pick up a prostitute. When I found one, we had a few drinks together and chatted, but it wasn't until we got into a cul-de-sac and started playing around that I told her I had never had sex with a woman. She was very understanding, but it wasn't until I closed my eyes and thought of Stuart that I was able to get an erection, and perform. I don't think she could have enjoyed it very much because I was so nervous. I know I didn't. Back in the public house I slipped a fiver into her bag, and then went to the toilet and left by the back way. Thinking about it on the way back to Eastdale, I felt dirty, and it wasn't until I had a long discussion with the psychologist that I felt easy in my own mind about what had taken place. The second time I went with a woman it didn't seem so awkward: I experienced less internal conflict when I was in a woman's company and gradually began to feel at ease.

Having discussed such personal matters with the psychologist, I wanted to make *her* feel committed to *me*, the way I had felt when I was revealing my innermost thoughts and feelings to her. I hated to think that she had uncovered my darkest secrets, so I went out of my way to embarrass her and to make her feel as exposed as I had. I decided that a social evening at the Festival Hall in Nottingham would be my golden opportunity. I asked her to dance and deliberately started dancing too close for comfort and moving my hands in awkward places. However, the plan backfired. Instead of embarrassing her in front of everyone, as I'd planned, I found that I was enjoying it, and afterwards she said 'Oh, at least you do fancy women then'.

I tried to get her to come out on a date with me, but she wouldn't wear it. In the light of this chain of events, the one-to-one therapy became a farce, in my opinion.

*　*　*

If my social rehabilitation was problematic, workwise everything was going well. My first few months at Eastdale were spent in the carpentry and joinery department of the training unit. Here people can learn the basic skills of carpentry, and go on to further training if they wish to continue in this trade. People who aren't suited to carpentry, as I wasn't, can take up engineering or gardening or join the concrete-making project. I found that I wasn't very keen on woodwork, so I talked things over with the charge nurse and Mr Kerr, the training officer, and it was agreed that I would be interviewed by the head porter at Balderton. If he accepted me, I would go to work on the portering staff.

I took to portering straight away, I think for two very good reasons. Firstly, I had a variety of jobs to do in and out of doors, and secondly I met new people, both male and female. This did me the world of good, and the more people I met, the more confidence I gained — confidence I badly needed if I was to stand any chance of making it when I left the unit. While on the portering staff, I only came across one person who tried his best to upset me and get me into trouble. He was an ex-Rampton staff who, in my opinion, should not be employed anywhere in the health service, such is his inhuman attitude towards his fellow man. I was not sorry to learn some years later that this person had in fact been discharged from the service.

Although I enjoyed the portering job very much, I knew I would soon have to move on because everyone on my regular case conference had agreed that I should go into the hospital laundry to work with the females. When the time came to change, I was a little apprehensive about working with nearly all women. Much to my surprise, however, I really enjoyed it, as I soon found out that working with women was a lot more fun than working with men. I would not have missed this experience for the world!

My stay in the laundry came to an abrupt end as I was accepted to go on an assessment course at Long Eaton Skill Centre. My first few days there were spent in the intake department, and they were very unsettling. Apparently even now I found it hard to accept change, but fortunately the staff there were very understanding and soon made me feel part of things. After that I settled in quite quickly, although it took me a good two weeks to get used to travelling there by bus and train; I was pleased I had another lad with me.

While at Long Eaton, I had various tests and found that I had far more potential than I had credited myself with. The days at the centre were long, but it helped me get used to rising at 6.00 am and working a full day until 5.00 pm. It also gave me a chance to get used to handling money as I received a weekly pay packet.

I really enjoyed the course and it was very beneficial in that it made me feel more confident about getting a job and, what's more important, holding down a steady post.

Christmas time came while I was still on the course. We were allowed five days holiday, and I was looking forward to my first Christmas out of Rampton in ten years. Being at Eastdale, a place where I had friends and was well liked, I thought that Christmas would come and go without any of the low periods I usually had at this time of year. However this was not to be. I had a good Christmas with my friends at Eastdale, yet by New Year's week I felt so lonely and low. I couldn't understand why, and was interviewed by the psychologist several times. On occasions she would get me so rattled that speaking with Dad was the only thing that settled me down.

* * *

After finishing at Long Eaton, I got my job back with the porters at Balderton, and I enjoyed it as much as I did the first time round. Not only did the porters accept me, they couldn't have been more helpful in preparing me for a day's work when the time came for me to leave Eastdale.

Between the portering job and football at weekends and my ward commitments, I began to feel a lot better about the social side of things. I started to feel that it was time for me to leave Eastdale: if I didn't go soon, I would become too reliant on the unit and wouldn't want to leave at all.

After my final case conference it was agreed that I could go and find a job and a flat, and then leave Eastdale under medical and social supervision, subject to Home Office approval. The only doubt I had in my mind, which I didn't reveal to anyone in case it stopped my release, was about how I would react if I came across any sort of trouble. I felt I would have to be whiter than white until I was accepted back into society.

I was told I couldn't resettle in Nottinghamshire, so I decided to try and get a job in Sheffield. I wrote off for four jobs, and the one I felt I stood the best chance of getting was a portering post at a mental hospital. As they knew all about the mental health system, I felt my application would get a fair hearing, and I came out of the interview with high hopes. However I soon received a letter telling me that because of my background I had been unsuccessful. I was shocked. Had I been turned down because they didn't think I was the right man for the job, I could have understood, but their attitude indicated that jobwise the whole of the Sheffield Health Authority area was out of the question.

I discussed my employment prospects with the training officer at Balderton, who suggested that I talk to a Disablement Resettlement Officer (DRO). I did so, and we discussed the possibility of me going on a GPO training course. However, the GPO declined to co-operate, even though I'd already had some training in this field at Long Eaton.

A portering post came up at Balderton Hospital, but while I was in the middle of applying for it, I was given authority to find a job in the Nottingham area, if I so wished. In the weeks that followed I spent a lot of time in Nottingham looking for a suitable job. I turned to the Job Centre for advice on vacancies in the area, and to my utter amazement I was told in no uncertain terms by the manager that the centre couldn't help 'my type of person'. If I required help, I would have to go to another office, register as disabled, and then see a Disablement Resettlement Officer. Until I told them about my background, they were willing to treat me like any other member of the public seeking employment, and what was just as annoying, they were prepared to go on strike rather than interview me. This episode made me feel so inhuman that I wondered whether ordinary members of the public would ever be able to accept me.

My confidence had taken such a battering that I gave up looking for work for a while, but after a few weeks I decided to give it one last try. If I failed this time, I was prepared to call it a day. I wrote off for three jobs which I'd seen advertised in a local newspaper. Two of the vacancies had already been taken, but the third, a porter's job at Mapperley Hospital, was still open. After a good deal of internal politicking behind the scenes, the head porter interviewed me and — to a lot of people's dismay — accepted me for the job on merit. I was so pleased: I really wanted to make a success of my portering career to thank those people who had helped me at Balderton, and to give something back. Having been on both sides of the hospital fence, so to speak, I have a much deeper insight and understanding of hospital life than most.

* * *

From the moment the job offer was confirmed, I had exactly two weeks to find myself a flat. Knowing that I had only a fortnight left at Eastdale, I felt so strange. I so much wanted to leave, yet for just over 13 months I had looked upon Eastdale as my first real home. My heart wasn't in the task of finding a flat, and I only accepted a place two days before I was due to leave Eastdale.

The last time I called a ward meeting as chairman, I was just pleased that my feelings didn't get the better of me. It was odd that I should be handing over the chairmanship to the person I had a special feeling for, but the others had voted him in, so it was all fair and above board. Looking back on it, passing this responsibility on to Stuart was a help to me in a funny sort of way.

I was to leave Eastdale on the Friday so that I could set up my flat over the weekend, and be ready to start work on the Monday. A party had been arranged at my local, *The Cock Inn,* for a few friends on the Thursday evening, so I made sure all my packing was done by Thursday lunchtime, leaving me the afternoon free to say my goodbyes.

What took place that afternoon couldn't have been foreseen, and deep down I wish so much it hadn't happened. One of the lads on Eastdale was so unsettled that he decided to take his own life; as I walked into the lounge I saw him through the window slashing his wrist and neck with a blade. I panicked and ran towards him, which in turn must have made *him* panic for he started running over the fields towards the railway lines. I kept calling out to him that I wanted to say goodbye as I was leaving, and kept trying to offer him a cigarette. This didn't do any good, and it wasn't until he was on the railway lines that I caught up with him. I pulled him off the line and kept talking to him while taking my shirt off to put round his neck, which looked one hell of a mess. I put my hands around his wrists to stop the blood, and then sat with him talking until help came. A train appeared in the distance, so I took hold of his hand while talking to him. He then asked for a cigarette, and without thinking I let him go and lit up two cigarettes. As I did this, the train came by, and he jumped up and rushed towards it. I pulled him back down the bank and didn't let go again until help arrived.

It wasn't until he had been escorted away, and I was on my way back to the unit in the nursing officer's car, that I began to feel the affects of this sorrowful episode. I say sorrowful, because I learned while talking to him that he had been detained in Moss Side for nine years. In all this time nothing had been done to help him come to terms with his problems, which prompted him to take such drastic action. This lack of insight into patients' problems isn't unique to Moss Side: from what I know about the special hospital system, Rampton is by far the worst offender in this respect.

Once I was back in my room at Eastdale, I realised that through this boy's misfortune I'd discovered what my reaction would be in an emotional crisis. The whole unit was upset by the events of the afternoon, and a special ward meeting was called.

*   *   *

By 6.30 it was time for my going-away party, but it wasn't until I'd had plenty to drink that I really got into the party mood.

Thursday night passed unknown to me, but Friday is a day I shall always remember. I had breakfast at 7.15 am as usual, then washed, shaved and changed into the clothing I was leaving in as well as finishing my last bit of packing. I felt terrible, not only through the drinking of the night before. I so much wanted to be a free man, yet the thought of leaving Eastdale, my home, terrified me. I was so afraid, oh God. The only way I could keep my spirits up was to tell myself that I could either face up to the loneliness of being on my own in a world where at least I could find some freedom, or I could have my loneliness back in Rampton. I had to accept the fact that all my life I would be making changes; loneliness had been, was, and might always be a part of my life, no matter where I was.

Everyone I spoke to wished me the best of luck, and then it was time for Paul to take me to Nottingham to live alone.

MAKING IT ALONE

Before Paul left he gave me his phone number in case I needed to get in touch with him at home, which was good of him. He had to leave quickly as he had another boy to take home. That was bad enough, but the worst part was saying goodbye to Stuart. He had been in Nottingham for the day and came to say his farewells and wish me the best. I tried so hard not to show how low I was really feeling as so many people had put their faith in me. Not to give myself a chance at this stage would be so stupid.

I kept myself busy for the first few hours by making my bed, paying the rent and going to the shops on the Mansfield Road for tea, sugar, milk, bread, butter and eggs. By 7.00 pm I had rung Dad and done everything else I could find to do, except unpack my belongings. Suddenly I felt so afraid and alone. Here I was in a house which seemed so quiet, so empty. I had never been on my own before, and it was horrible. I went to bed and cried myself to sleep.

The worst thing I found upon waking up next morning was that it was so quiet. There was no noise, not even any music; it was so quiet and unreal that I started talking to myself just to hear a sound. I got up at about 7.00 am, and after making my bed and having breakfast I went to the shop for some cigarettes.

I had a wonderful surprise when I got back: Paul had brought his wife and son to visit me. I think God must have answered my prayers — I had never been so happy to see friends in all my life. The half-hour they spent with me made me feel so great, it was mind-blowing. I knew I couldn't spend the rest of the weekend on my own, so I rang Keith, a friend who had been at Eastdale and was now living in an after-care hostel in Chesterfield. I spoke to the gentleman in charge of the hostel; he was very understanding and kind, and invited me over to the hostel for the weekend. Don I now consider to be a friend I will always respect and hold in high esteem. He is one of the few people who knew the worst about me, yet he was prepared to meet me and to get to know me before he judged me.

Without the kindness and help of Don and Keith, and the continuing friendship of Dad and others at Eastdale, it would have taken me a lot longer to come to terms with my new life. As it was, it was a good year after I left the unit before I began to feel really settled in society.

* * *

When I came back to the flat on Sunday, I had two nasty shocks in store. First, I didn't know how to set the alarm clock I had bought at the weekend. I had never used one and I was not about to ask my landlady, although I knew she would have helped me, so I decided to keep awake to make sure I wasn't late for my first day at work. The second and most stupid thing was that I didn't know how to work the meter so the electricity went off. The landlady had shown me how to do it when I first moved in, but I'd forgotten. I felt such a fool: a man of 35 with no idea how to set an alarm or work a meter. I felt so inadequate and so alone, I could have died.

I dozed during Sunday night, but was up making tea at 6.00 am and on my way by 6.35. I felt so light-headed and proud, but by the time I got there I was a nervous wreck. I knew the head porter and some of the administration staff were aware of my background, and knowing how well hospital grapevines work, I wondered what kind of story might have got around about me. I met the other porters during the day and have since learned that they are a good lot. Some guessed I had an odd past, some I told, yet I never had a wrong word said to me.

For the first week or two the other porters took me around the hospital to show me the different places where I was to work, and told me what my duties were. Being a domestic porter rather than a general porter meant my duties covered a wide range of jobs, which made it most interesting. The only drawback to being on the domestic side was that there was no daily contact with the patients, and consequently less feeling of achievement at the end of the day.

*　　*　　*

About a week after I started, I was walking along the main corridor with a chargehand porter when a familiar voice shouted: 'Harding, have you got a fag?'. I turned to see Eddie, who had been in Rampton with me, and before I could take control of the situation he continued: 'We were in Rampton together . . . give us a smoke'. Thinking quickly, I said: 'Yes Eddie, you can have a cigarette, but I'd like you to know that I now work here, not in Rampton, and live in Nottingham'. I felt I had to make such a statement because there were quite a lot of people walking up and down the corridor; I wanted people to get to know me and form an opinion of me before my past was too widely known. At the end of the day I wanted to make a career out of portering, and I was all too aware that I was still on trial. Like all new staff I had to work a three month trial period, and my services could still be dispensed with at any time. I knew that the hospital had broken a golden rule by giving me the job in the first place — it's not common practice to accept a former special hospital patient for a health service post. To some extent this is understandable from a public relations point of view, but if health authorities aren't prepared to accept ex-patients from Rampton, how can you expect ordinary employers to be sympathetic?

*　　*　　*

My first few months at work were enjoyable. I knew I had picked the right career, but my home life was a nightmare. Out of sheer loneliness I kept ringing friends at Eastdale and elsewhere just so that I had someone to talk to. The silence in the flat and simply being alone was unnerving for someone who had spent 34 years in institutions of one kind or another. I thought I was taking the easy way out by getting another job in the evenings, but I soon found that there is no permanent escape in this way. Within a short time the strain of settling into society and doing two jobs took its toll. I woke up one morning feeling absolutely lifeless and I suddenly knew that there was something very wrong with me. I got up slowly and dressed with difficulty, but I'd only taken three steps outside my room when I felt a sudden terrific burning pain in my chest, and stumbled to the floor. It took me about half an hour to get from my room to the flat next door, and by the time I got there I had lost the use of my left arm. I'm still not sure what it was, although it was put down to a minor heart attack.

While I was on sick leave, the authorities at Mapperley couldn't have been more helpful, which was more than could be said for the DHSS. I hadn't claimed sickness benefit for years, of course, so the local social security office helped me fill in the right form and sent if off to the appropriate department. I didn't have to wait long for a reply. To my amazement — and other people's — I was told that I wasn't entitled to benefit because there were no records on me. Once some records were found, or new ones made out, they would write to me again. I did eventually receive some money a few weeks later, but this didn't cover my rent for a lot of the time I was off work.

Needless to say, I gave up my part-time job.

*   *   *

After three years at Mapperley, I decided to go after promotion. I knew I could be 25 years in the hospital service, and aimed to become first a chargehand porter and then deputy head porter. I was well aware that such ambitions would be frowned on in certain quarters — in some circles the fact that I was on the staff at all didn't go down at all well. What would happen if I was in any form of authority? I decided this wasn't going to stop me, and after three unsuccessful attempts I became deputy head porter — much to some people's amazement. It was very hard work at first, but as I gained more insight into what the job was about I really started to enjoy the challenge. I went to college and passed my City & Guilds Part 1 exam in cleaning science — an achievement I'm very proud of.

*   *   *

I went into Rampton as a restricted patient — which meant that the Home Office had to approve my transfer or discharge. Even out in society I was still under this restriction order and the Home Office could recall me to Rampton at any time. In my opinion, this system of recall does much more harm than good. Can you imagine the effect of resettling into society under this unwanted strain? The Home Office is not accountable, and the former patient has no say in the matter.

About three years after I'd left Eastdale, I applied to have my restriction order lifted. Whether it was because I have a first class solicitor or because I'd become very involved in promoting the rights of patients in Rampton I don't know, but the order was lifted without argument. This is most unusual: ex-special hospital patients aren't normally considered until they've been back in society for at least five years.

THE SECRET HOSPITAL

Until the late 1970s, most members of the public knew little — and cared less — about what went on in Rampton. All that changed when Yorkshire Television made *The Secret Hospital,* the film that took the lid off Rampton and shocked the nation. I'm proud and honoured that I was able to play such a big part in the making of this documentary.

I was at Eastdale when the idea of the film first came up. Arriving back from Long Eaton Skill Centre one Friday, I found a man from Yorkshire Television at the unit asking questions. He wanted to do a programme about Eastdale, and my first reaction was not on your life! The press and TV have always made life even harder for those of us who are or have been in mental hospitals, and Eastdale had already had a hammering in the press. For the first and only time I used my position as ward chairman to quietly persuade others to veto the idea of the programme when we had a ward meeting to discuss it. On the day of the meeting, Dr Hunter was there and so were John Willis and James Cutler from YTV. They answered all our questions very openly, and stated that if the programme did go ahead, everyone taking part would have a written contract. No-one would have to say anything they didn't want to and — most importantly — those who chose not to take part in the programme would be left alone. They were very reassuring and many of us, including me, changed our minds and agreed that a programme *should* be made about the Eastdale unit. Little did I know at this time that they would use me in the programme so much.

A few weeks into the filming, John and James proposed that the film should focus on me, and follow my progress through Eastdale and out into society. It was a big decision for me, but I eventually agreed to be singled out on the condition that YTV would also take a look at Rampton. I remember saying: 'You don't have to promise to *do* anything, but just take a look'. They did — and *The Secret Hospital* was the result.

When I agreed to take part in the programme I had no thought of financial gain. For years the biased attitudes and lack of insight of the media have done untold harm to patients. Headlines like 'Madman on the loose' — or worse — give the public a totally false impression. They learn to fear the mental patient, and therefore don't mind what sort of care the patient receives as long as he's out of the way.

★　★　★

88

The programme-makers followed my last months in Eastdale, and while I was settling into my new way of life in the community YTV was still filming every move I made. However, I'd have to say that they were my least concern, for it was a full-time effort for me to adjust to living in society. In some ways the filming interfered with my job: it meant that I had to take time off work, which I could have done without, and it also meant that they filmed me in Mapperley which would surely start the hospital grapevine buzzing with questions — the last thing I wanted at this time.

All told, filming took about nine months, and as the date the programmes were to be shown drew near, I became more and more worried. Rampton staff were naturally less than pleased about what was going on, and there were suggestions that John Willis, James Cutler and I would be got at as a result of *The Secret Hospital* and *The Way Out* (the film on Eastdale). Two or three weeks previous to the showing of the two films, I was followed home from work on three occasions. I reported this to my social worker, for I had no idea why I should have been followed. One evening I came out of my flat with someone from YTV, and saw a person I thought was on the Rampton staff. I panicked and ran back into the flat, and after talking it over with my lady friend Jean, rang the police.

The first of the two films, *The Secret Hospital,* was shown on Tuesday 23 May 1979, and I was due to attend the press showing the day before. I didn't like the idea of Jean being alone in the flat, so we agreed that she would stop with friends until the weekend.

*   *   *

I was so nervous on the morning of the press showing, it was like waiting for the verdict after an interview. Although I had seen parts of the films, I hadn't seen the finished programmes, and there were times when I wished YTV hadn't been there with their cameras. The films could do a lot of good — or more harm. I began to have doubts. Had I done the right thing by being so open and honest? It was too late to do anything about it now.

I sat in the front row with James, and as more and more members of the press and people from organisations like MIND and NCCL came in, I felt sick with nerves. I needn't have worried. The reaction was overwhelming, and I could hear hardened press people gasping with shock and dismay. Taking everything into consideration, I felt that YTV had given a very good insight into what Rampton was like. Thinking about it in the interval between the two films, I decided it was perhaps a good thing that *The Secret Hospital* hadn't revealed *more* of the truth about Rampton, for that would have served no purpose apart from tarnishing decent staff with the same brush as the others. A big part of the second film, *The Way Out,* was focused on me: I couldn't believe what I was seeing — I wished the camera work hadn't been so good. I told John and James that I'd prefer them to leave out at least two incidents in the film, but it went out on television as the press had seen it.

The two days after the films were shown on TV, I took part in television and radio programmes from London to Manchester. In fact I did so much TV and radio work that I gained a very good impression of how the films had been received by the public, and I felt it was well worth all the worry I'd had. I was a seven day wonder, and I was pleased that my moment of celebrity was so brief, for it was the wider issues which needed attention, not me. The interviews I did gave me an ideal opportunity to put across my views on the special hospital system, but the main question everyone asked me was: 'What do you enjoy most in life now you're back in society?'. My answer was always the same, and I hope I will always feel this way: 'Just to be able to walk down any road and see people from all walks of life enjoying themselves in their own way gives me so much happiness and contentment. It seems to me that when you've had freedom all your life, instead of using it well, you tend to abuse it by taking it for granted. I'm lucky — I get so much from my walks every day'.

Once the fuss had died down a bit, I went home to Jean. It was so nice to be home: I was still high on my nerves and needed to relax. Jean was marvellous; she kept answering the door and phone and took charge of everything because she knew I was worried about the reaction I'd get from people at Mapperley when I went back to work on Monday. In the event, the reaction was mixed. I'd just been made up to pharmacy porter (which meant a little more money and responsibility), and one of my Monday morning jobs was to collect the medical boxes from all the wards. I therefore had no chance of keeping a low profile, as I would have wished. Most of the domestic porters treated me quite normally, however, although some of the other staff in the hospital felt I might have cast the whole of the health service profession into disrepute. I think there could be very little justification for this accusation, because YTV stated quite clearly that the programmes concerned the special hospital system only — thank God very few local mental hospitals are run like Rampton. Apart from this initial reaction, very little comment was passed, which allowed me to continue with my work without too many problems. I was so pleased that it turned out like this, for I loved my job.

*　　*　　*

In my opinion the public response to both YTV films has been very positive in the sense that a lot more good than harm has been done since. The Home Office and the DHSS are beginning to accept their legal and moral responsibility for the way Rampton is run, but they still have a long way to go.

The programmes caused such a stir that there was a televised debate on the Rampton issue, and following this former patients, members of NCCL, solicitors and other interested parties set up a group called PROPAR which stands for Protection of the Rights of Patients at Rampton. I was asked if I would like to join, and I agreed immediately. I felt there was a real need for such an organisation: MIND and the NCCL have been working on behalf of psychiatric patients for years, but their attempts to help patients in institutions like Rampton have always been blocked. YTV had made public the plight of special hospital patients and their families; here was a golden opportunity to put things right.

Yorkshire Television loaned PROPAR a copy of both *The Secret Hospital* and *The Way Out*, and we took the films all over the country to universities, colleges and other interested bodies. I gave a talk after the films were shown, and then answered the audience's questions. There was never any shortage of questions, and the most common one was this: 'What is the worst problem with Rampton, and who is to blame?'. Most people were taken aback at my answer: 'I condemn not the violence or the misuse of power at Rampton, but the attitude of many Rampton staff and the DHSS and the Home Office in London. No matter what reforms are introduced, until attitudes change Rampton will always be a backward unholy place for the patients and for decent staff. Under these circumstances, it is in everyone's interest that Rampton be closed down'.

With the help of MIND and NCCL, PROPAR has achieved a lot through demonstrations, complaints to the Queen and MPs, and use of the press. We aim to make Rampton a respectable and caring hospital in accordance with the human rights laws, or to have it closed down completely — as many secret reports have suggested should happen. Over a three year period I spent some of my annual holidays and days off working for PROPAR, and I consider that it was well worth the time and effort, if nothing else just to get people to stop and think about mental illness — the illness no-one really accepts or understands.

*　　*　　*

The public outrage started by the YTV programmes and continued by PROPAR resulted in a police enquiry into brutality at Rampton, and to my amazement, I found my faith in the British police restored. While I was in Rampton I found that the local police were extremely biased against patients, and they displayed exactly the same attitude towards PROPAR when we were demonstrating outside the hospital. I thought the enquiry would be a whitewash, but I was proved wrong. The Nottinghamshire police involved in the investigation couldn't have been more impartial and thorough, although they had to work under very trying circumstances. I learned a good lesson: never judge the whole for what parts may do.

The committal proceedings took place in Mansfield; the trials in Leicester, Lincoln and Nottingham. I attended them all, and it's a pity that other departments in our legal system couldn't be as fair and just as the Nottinghamshire police. The court cases more than justified the campaign to open up Rampton, but what PROPAR wanted was an independent public enquiry. We knew there had been several secret reports over the years recommending sweeping changes, but *none* of the recommendations has ever been implemented except the suggestion that children under the age of 16 should be moved out.

However, we got our way, and the Boynton committee was set up to consider Rampton and its future. Like the other official documents before it, the Boynton committee's report recommended sweeping changes, and stated that Rampton should be closed down if the major recommendations had not been implemented within three years. The report was accepted by the Home Office, the DHSS, parliament, the British Medical Association and the Prison Officers' Association (the union Rampton nurses belong to) at the end of 1980, but *none* of the major recommendations has been implemented. The three year deadline is long gone, but Rampton is still there, and even a former medical director has stated that the place should be closed. One staff convicted of causing grievous bodily harm to a patient by breaking his jaw has already got his job back: is this not final proof that Rampton is above the law? Nowhere else in private or government service could a person commit such acts and then get his job back after three years on full pay. Patients sent to court for attacking staff are detained for *25 years*, yet staff found guilty of violence against patients receive little or no punishment, proving that the system is against the person who is ill. I wonder what decent people think about this. How long must we treat our psychiatric patients worse than animals? There but for the grace of God go any of us.

Despite all this, I truly believe that if attitudes were to change and the Boynton report was fully implemented, Rampton could become the leading hospital of its kind in this country, if not the world. *That* is the saddest thing in this awful situation.

JEAN

In describing my new life in society, I've deliberately left the best till last — and Jean is far and away the best thing that's ever happened to me. I met her on an outing to a working man's club in Bilsthorpe while I was still at Eastdale, and we dated for about two months. Jean had very little idea of what Eastdale was about, and knew nothing about my background except that I was a batchelor and a FA referee. I took her out twice on my own for a meal and a show, otherwise we always met at the club. Jean was married with a son, and while we enjoyed each other's company, it would have been totally wrong, for both our sakes, for me to continue with the relationship until I had begun to sort out the problems that come with resettling into society after so many years. I was also uncertain about whether or not I could cope with a deeper relationship

* * *

I decided it was best to break off the relationship for a while, and didn't come into contact with Jean again until the period when I was on sick leave from Mapperley. Quite by chance I met a friend of Jean's who asked me how she was, and said to give her their regards. I still had her number, so I rang her a couple of days later and at the end of the call we arranged to meet the following week. It was to be the best phone call I would ever make! After this first meeting we agreed to meet at my flat each Saturday, and as the weeks went by we started to spend long weekends together. Neither Jean nor I felt any guilt, for her husband must have known what was taking place and I wasn't married. I got on well with Jean's son which meant I wouldn't be breaking up a complete family should our relationship become permanent.

I was still a restricted patient at this stage, and had to see Dr Hunter at Eastdale each month as part of my condition of licence. He naturally asked me about my work and my social life. When I told him parts about Jean and me, he was more than happy with how I was getting on. At times like this it's in one's interest not to go into too much detail!

Suddenly everything was going right for me. There had been no problems workwise, and now that my social life was at last coming together, I began to feel more secure in society. The next big testing point was telling Jean everything about myself, and I *mean* everything, including the tragic episode I have only touched on in this book. If there was going to be any chance of a long and stable relationship, Jean had to know the truth before the film came on television, and before our relationship became too deep. I shall never forget that Saturday afternoon in my flat when I broke my past to Jean. There was no gentle way to tell her, and the shock on her face couldn't be disguised. I left her crying while I made a pot of tea. As if that wasn't enough of a shock for one day, I then had to inform her that I had been filming with YTV and that the programme would be shown nationwide within a few months. It was important for Jean to understand the situation fully and to have the opportunity to consider whether she wanted to continue with our relationship, given that she had a home, a son and husband and a job she enjoyed in Bilsthorpe. It was a decision she and only she could make. I answered all her questions about my past and the future, but couldn't predict what the outcome of the two documentaries might be.

I asked Jean to think over the whole matter and let me know her decision during the next week. However, to my amazement and delight, she told me she loved me and was looking forward to the day we would be living together permanently. The relief I felt was so great, and we both sat weeping with joy.

Our relationship grew over the next few months, and I started looking for a bigger flat. It was the happiest day of my life when Jean moved in with me and the long lonely periods of my life seemed to vanish. At long last I belonged; I was part of a two way love, and I had someone who cared for me and wanted to share her life with me. There is no greater happiness.

*   *   *

After a while we decided to get married, and Jean put in for a divorce. We knew it would take time, and perhaps this was a good thing for what with my work, refereeing, and PROPAR commitments, I was spending far less time at home with Jean than I would have wished. I gave up refereeing, but still found I was spending the same amount of time away from home. We were therefore so pleased when Jean gained a domestic post at Mapperley: we were able to see more of each other, and going to work together made the day more enjoyable. While PROPAR is still very involved in helping patients and their relatives, I don't spend so much time away from home now, which both Jean and I are more than happy about.

Jean's divorce came through without any bitterness or anyone getting hurt, so we started making arrangements for what was supposed to be a quiet registry office wedding. As it turned out, the wedding was anything but quiet! The local press were on the doorstep wanting interviews, John and James from YTV were there, and John stood in as our best man as unfortunately the friend who should have been the best man couldn't make it till later. Some of our domestic colleagues turned up in their uniforms and made an archway with their mops and brushes as we came out of the registry office. We were so surprised! It was a wonderful day, and we were thankful to our friends and colleagues who were there for making it so great. When we got home there was yet another surprise in store. We had intended to have just a few drinks, but our next-door neighbours had arranged a lovely wedding reception for us.

We had a few days off work, and stayed at our new home, number 9. I wondered what the future would hold.

EPILOGUE

After our marriage, Jean and I increased our mortgage on our new home, and got a local authority grant to modernise our property. Unfortunately the work was done completely wrong, and for the first time in my life I knew what it's like to be in debt. To add to our problems, Jean's health became so poor that she had to retire from work, and within two years I too had to retire from my hard-earned position as deputy head porter after an accident at work.

This was probably the most difficult time for me since leaving Eastdale. I knew Jean had health problems when we first met, but I had foreseen myself being in the portering service for at least 20 years, not just seven. For a time I didn't think I'd be able to overcome the problems caused by these changes and uncertainty, but with Jean's help I pulled through it.

We have had to sell number 9, but we have a lovely new home with a little garden. We are still very much in love and very happy, and we are looking forward to the future together.